HOW TO RAISE VENTURE CAPITAL

HOW TO RAISE VENTURE CAPITAL

Stanley E. Pratt
&
the Editors of
VENTURE CAPITAL JOURNAL

CHARLES SCRIBNER'S SONS · NEW YORK

Copyright © 1982, 1981, 1977, 1974, 1972, 1970
by Capital Publishing Corporation

Library of Congress Cataloging in Publication Data

Guide to venture capital sources.
How to raise venture capital.

Originally published, with a directory, as:
Guide to venture capital sources. 5th ed.
Wellesley Hills, Mass. : Capital Pub. Corp, c1981.
Includes index.
   1. Venture capital—United States. 2. Small business—United States—Finance. I. Pratt, Stanley E. II. Venture capital journal.
HG4027.7.G84   1982   658.1'522   82-3393
ISBN 0-684-17444-8   AACR2

This book published simultaneously in the
United States of America and in Canada—
Copyright under the Berne Convention

All rights reserved. No part of this book
may be reproduced in any form without the
permission of Charles Scribner's Sons.

1 3 5 7 9 11 13 15 17 19 F/C 20 18 16 14 12 10 8 6 4 2

Printed in the United States of America.

How to Raise Venture Capital *is also published by Capital Publishing Corporation as part of the book* Guide to Venture Capital Sources, *and is reprinted here by permission.*

Copyright © 1970, 1972, 1974, 1977, and 1981 by Capital Publishing Corporation.

Contents

Contributors	vii
FOREWORD	xiii
PREFACE	xv
INTRODUCTION	1
BACKGROUND	7

Overview and Introduction to the Venture Capital Industry   9
   STANLEY E. PRATT
Characteristics of a Successful Entrepreneur   15
   ALEXANDER L. M. DINGEE, JR.,
   LEONARD E. SMOLLEN, and BRIAN HASLETT

SOURCES OF BUSINESS DEVELOPMENT FINANCING   27

The Organized Venture Capital Community   29
   STANLEY E. PRATT
Informal Investors—When and Where to Look   36
   WILLIAM E. WETZEL, JR.
Pre-Startup Seed Capital   47
   WILLIAM R. CHANDLER
SBA Programs for Financing a Small Business   54
   DAVID J. GLADSTONE
Community Development Corporations and Economic Development Commissions   63
   FREDERICK J. BESTE III
The MESBIC Connection: Venture Capital for the Forgotten Entrepreneur   72
   WALTER M. MCMURTRY, JR.
Corporate Venture Capital   77
   KENNETH W. RIND

HOW TO RAISE VENTURE CAPITAL   85

Guidelines for Dealing with Venture Capitalists   87
   STANLEY E. PRATT

Preparing a Business Plan 95
BRIAN HASLETT and LEONARD E. SMOLLEN
The Presentation and Other Key Elements 121
CHARLES P. WAITE
Venture Financing Techniques 127
EDWARD F. GLASSMEYER
Structuring and Pricing the Financing 134
STANLEY C. GOLDER
Legal Documents of Venture Financing 157
ROBERT R. MACDONALD and RICHARD J. TESTA, ESQ.
Venture Capital in Practice: A Case History 178
TIMOTHY M. PENNINGTON
The Key to Successful Leveraged Buyouts:
Analysis of Management 187
GREGORY P. BARBER

WHEN AND HOW TO GO PUBLIC 195

Public Financing for Smaller Companies 197
PETER W. WALLACE
Financial Public Relations—A Key Ingredient After
Going Public 206
EDWARD G. NOVOTNY
Management's Responsibilities Change When a
Company Becomes Publicly Held 218
BELMONT TOWBIN

PERSPECTIVES 221

The Art of Venturing 223
FREDERICK R. ADLER
Pitfalls in Venturing 229
ALAN PATRICOF
The Entrepreneur's Perspective 234
DONALD J. KRAMER
The Relationship Between Venture Capitalist and
Entrepreneur 243
BROOK H. BYERS

INDEX 249

Contributors

FREDERICK R. ADLER is a senior partner of the law firm of Reavis & McGrath, New York City, and is the managing general partner of Adler & Company, a venture capital firm also located in New York City. In the late 1960s Adler became intrigued with venture capital and began investing in early-stage ventures that are primarily technological. Since then, Mr. Adler has invested in about fifty enterprises, perhaps the most successful being Data General Corp., now the nation's second largest independent minicomputer manufacturer. Mr. Adler is considered an entrepreneur in the venture capital field.

GREGORY P. BARBER joined Narragansett Capital Corporation, Providence, Rhode Island, the nation's largest publicly held small business investment company, as a vice-president in October 1978. He is responsible for new investments and marketing. Prior to joining Narragansett, Mr. Barber was a vice-president in the National Accounts Division at Industrial National Bank of Rhode Island. He holds a Bachelor of Arts degree from Boston College.

FREDERICK J. BESTE III is president of Kentucky Highlands Investment Corporation, a community development corporation located in London, Kentucky. This firm is recognized as a leading advocate and successful example of the venture capital approach to establishing businesses in economically underdeveloped areas. Before joining Kentucky Highlands in 1975, Mr. Beste was vice-president of Greater Washington Investors, Inc., a publicly held venture capital firm located in Washington, D.C., which he joined in 1968.

BROOK H. BYERS is a general partner of Kleiner, Perkins, Caufield & Byers in San Francisco, California. Prior to KPC&B, he managed an SBIC for Asset Management Company (AMC), where he developed the style described in this article. Before associating with AMC, he worked in management positions for two publicly owned venture-backed companies in publishing and electronics. He received a BEE from Georgia Tech and an MBA from the Stanford Graduate School of Business. KPC&B manages a large venture capital investment fund and portfolio.

WILLIAM R. CHANDLER is a cofounder and general partner of the Bay Venture Group, San Francisco, a company specializing in startup and seed capital investment for new venture development. Before organizing Bay Venture in 1976, Mr. Chandler had been active as a venture capitalist and in operating management responsibilities for the prior 20 years.

ALEXANDER L. M. DINGEE, JR., is a cofounder and president of Venture Founders Corporation, Waltham, Massachusetts, and directs the investment activities of Business Development Group 1981 (BDG '81), a venture capital fund dedicated to investing in seed and start-up situations. Previously he successfully started two companies, both of which were sold for capital gain.

DAVID J. GLADSTONE is executive vice-president of Allied Capital Corporation, Washington, D.C., a publicly owned financial holding company with four wholly owned subsidiaries. Allied Investment Corporation is one of the nation's oldest Small Business Investment Companies which makes equity-type investments in small growth-oriented companies. Allied Lending Corporation is a participating lender with the U.S. Small Business Administration and makes guaranteed loans to small business concerns. Allied Development Corporation makes loans under the Farmers Home Administration as well as other government guaranteed loan programs. Allied Advisory, Inc., is a consulting business which provides assistance to small company managements.

EDWARD F. GLASSMEYER is a general partner of Oak Investment Partners, Westport, Connecticut, a $60 million venture capital limited partnership. Prior to forming Oak, Mr. Glassmeyer was president of Charter Oak Enterprises and was formerly managing partner of Sprout Capital Group after having been associated with Citicorp's venture capital group.

STANLEY C. GOLDER is a general partner of Golder, Thoma & Co., Chicago, Illinois, a $60 million venture capital fund founded in 1980. For the prior nine years he was president of the Equity Group of First Chicago Corp., one of the largest and most successful bank holding company business development investment affiliates, with assets over $100 million. He is a past president of both the National Association of Small Business Investment Companies and the National Venture Capital Association. Golder, Thoma & Co. is an active investor with a diversified investment philosophy.

BRIAN HASLETT is a cofounder and vice-president of Venture Founders Corporation and managing director of its new British subsidiary, Venture Founders Limited. He played a leading role in many of the new businesses Venture Founders Corporation helped create and finance. He has served as a contributing editor to VENTURE CAPITAL JOURNAL since 1977. Previously he was with Arthur D. Little, Inc.

DONALD J. KRAMER is president and chief executive officer of Hendrix Electronics, Inc., Manchester, New Hampshire, a venture capital financed manufacturer of text management systems, video display terminals, and optical character recognition scanners. His career has included positions at Crucible Steel, Star Market, and EG&G before he became directly involved with venture capital developments. In 1970, he became chief financial officer of Modicon Corporation, a company backed by a number of venture capitalists which manufactured and sold programmable controllers and other process control equipment. He became president of Modicon in 1973 and joined Gould, Inc., as a vice-president when that company acquired Modicon in 1977. He became president of Hendrix in 1978 at the request of its venture capital backers. Few entrepreneurs have had as diverse experience with venture capital investors as Kramer and he has served on the board of directors of numerous venture capital financed companies. He offers insight and observations about entrepreneur/venture capital relationships.

ROBERT R. MACDONALD is presently pursuing entrepreneurial rewards as president of Lifeline Systems, Inc., Waltham, Massachusetts, a venture-backed company which markets home-based medical electronics to hospitals and social service agencies. He was formerly a general partner of Idanta Partners, La Jolla, California, a leading private venture capital firm.

WALTER M. MCMURTRY, JR., is a founder and president of the Inner-City Business Improvement Forum (ICBIF), Detroit, one of the largest minority business development corporations in the U.S. Since 1973 he has also served as president of its subsidiary, Independence Capital Formation, Inc. He is a director and past president of the American Association of MESBICS and participates in the Economic Development Administration's Financial Roundtable as well as numerous other federal, state and city commissions.

EDWARD G. NOVOTNY is president of Fred Rosen Associates, Inc., a New York City headquartered corporate and financial public relations firm.

ALAN PATRICOF is chairman of Alan Patricof Associates, Inc., New York City. The firm was started in December 1969, and although it occasionally finances startup projects, most of its investments are in ongoing businesses. Alan Patricof Associates is particularly known for its activity in consumer, communications, publishing, and industrial oriented ventures. The firm primarily organizes ventures that are funded by in-house pools of capital.

TIMOTHY M. PENNINGTON is a general partner of Brentwood Associates, Los Angeles, a venture capital firm active in a wide range of investments, from startups to established companies, as well as special situations. Mr. Pennington, originally an engineer, has been involved with venture capital and corporate finance since 1966. In 1972 he left the investment banking firm of Blyth & Co. as a vice-president to join Brentwood Associates at its formation.

STANLEY E. PRATT is president of Capital Publishing Corporation and editor of its monthly publication, VENTURE CAPITAL JOURNAL, which has been reporting and analyzing business development investing since 1961. Mr. Pratt is also a managing director of Venture Economics, the research information services and consulting division of Capital Publishing Corporation. An active venture capitalist prior to assuming his present responsibilities in 1977, Mr. Pratt has become recognized as a leading authority on the venture capital industry.

KENNETH W. RIND is a general partner of Oxford Partners, Greenwich, Connecticut, which manages venture capital funds provided by corporate and financially oriented investors. Prior to that, he was a principal of Xerox Development Corporation, the corporate development and venture capital subsidiary of Xerox Corporation.

LEONARD E. SMOLLEN is executive vice-president, a cofounder of Venture Founders Corporation, and involved with Alexander L. M. Dingee, Jr., in the startup and seed venture investment activities of BDG '81. He previously held executive positions at EG&G, Inc.

RICHARD J. TESTA is a partner in the Boston law firm of Testa, Hurwitz & Thibeault. He and his firm have served as counsel for several professional venture capital companies as well as for a large number of businesses that have been financed by venture capital sources.

BELMONT TOWBIN is a limited partner in L. F. Rothschild, Unterberg, Towbin investment bankers in New York City. The firm's corporate finance department specializes in raising capital for emerging growth companies.

CHARLES P. WAITE was a founder of Greylock & Co., Boston, Massachusetts, a family venture firm, of which he is currently a general partner. Greylock has been an active venture firm for many years, and its key principals have been associated with the venture capital business since the early 1950s. The firm tends to prefer technology situations, but is careful to be involved in only a few startups at any single period. Most Greylock investments are in ongoing businesses, or in second-stage situations. He has been a teaching assistant of General Doriot at Harvard Business School and is a frequent guest lecturer at HBS and at Dartmouth's Tuck School. He was an officer at American Research and Development Corporation (ARD) for a number of years.

PETER WALLACE is a general partner of Hambrecht & Quist, San Francisco, California. His background includes eighteen years in investment banking and venture capital with J. Barth & Co., White Weld & Co., Hale Bros. Associates, and Wallace & Schilling; before that he was manager of the product development division of Raychem Corporation. Hambrecht & Quist is an investment banking partnership primarily serving emerging companies with substantial growth potential. The firm provides a full range of investment banking services to its corporate clients and is not only a leading underwriter of securities for emerging growth companies, but is also a major factor in the venture capital financing of early-stage companies.

WILLIAM E. WETZEL is Professor of Finance at the Whittemore School of Business and Economics at the University of New Hampshire in Durham. With sponsorship from the Office of Economic Research of the U.S. Small Business Administration he is currently directing a study, conducted by the Center for Industrial and Institutional Development at UNH, to look at the cost and availability of informal risk capital in New England. The emphasis of this study is upon firms without access to traditional venture capital sources or the public equity markets.

Foreword

The title of this book brings back many memories. In 1923 I had a good idea, but no money. The New England textile industry at that time had over 19 million cotton spindles in place and was beginning to use the new, synthetic fibers like rayon and Celanese in their fabrics. The dyeing and processing of these yarns was being done by real silk operators in Pennsylvania and New Jersey. I thought that a company to do this work in New England would have a genuine advantage and could be unusually successful.

A good friend, Eliot Farley, endorsed a ten-thousand-dollar note for Special Yarns Corporation, and we started in leased space in South Boston, without any equity capital.

The first year our sales were only $75,000 with a profit of $3,600. Within a couple of years our volume exceeded $1 million, but because of lack of equity, we had to factor our accounts receivable and also borrow against our inventories. The result was that these high interest and factoring costs offset most of our earnings.

In 1925, we found a wealthy friend who bought 20 percent of our shares, for $100,000, and from then on we made progress.

In 1928 we merged with a Providence company, resulting in our stockholders having 50 percent of the common stock of the surviving corporation. I personally had to raise $250,000 for our half of a $500,000 senior preferred issue. I went to a good friend who was an investment banker in Boston, hoping to raise this money from the public, but he turned me down, saying that the merger looked to him like two drunks trying to help each other home. I finally had to persuade friends and relatives to put up that money.

In 1936, when our sales were $5.5 million, a small investment banking firm did raise $500,000 for the company by selling common stock. Then in 1944, when we had converted the company to a completely integrated producer of consumer products—and had changed the name to Textron—we did our first significant public financing, a $2 million, 5 percent convertible debenture issue with additional warrants at a time when our total net worth was about $2 million. From then on we never had trouble raising capital from many different sources.

As a result of this twenty-year struggle raising capital for my small business, I decided in 1959—three years before my retirement from Textron—to start an SBIC [Small Business Investment Company], Narragansett Capital Corporation, to assist other entrepreneurs in financing their startup businesses. We raised $5 million through a public offering, and Narragansett Capital has now become the largest publicly owned small business investment company in the country, having been financially involved in 130 different enterprises.

The entrepreneur of today, with a reasonable prospect of success in a new business, will not have the problems that I had in starting Textron. Since January 1980 over $1 billion has been put into limited partnerships in this country to assist entrepreneurs in financing their new operations. Therefore, it will not take them twenty years before they get substantial financial assistance.

—Royal Little
Past chairman,
Narragansett Capital Corporation

Preface

The United States was founded and has thrived on the principles of entrepreneurship and individual and collective risktaking. In many ways, the nation owes its development to the willingness of entrepreneurs and investors to assume the major risks inherent in new business development. The imagination, boldness, and energy of entrepreneurs and small business owners, combined with the persistence and involvement of experienced venture capital investors, has often led to the creation of new industries and new technologies, which in turn have increased the productivity of the nation's economic process and of its workers. If the nation is to perpetuate its history of growing economic affluence, it must continue to nurture the traditions of individual capitalism. In the spirit of revitalizing these traditions, this book is dedicated to those men and women who are willing to make the personal sacrifices required to build significant businesses, and to those venture capitalists with the skills, fortitude, and foresight to participate in new business development.

The relationship between the entrepreneur and the venture capitalist is often the key element in a successful venture and understanding this unique relationship is a necessary first step for the prospective entrepreneur. The entrepreneur brings fresh ideas and personal commitment to this relationship, while the venture capitalist brings financial backing and extremely valuable new business development experience. Although the entrepreneur and the operating management team are theoretically the critical elements in the relationship (since the venture capitalist cannot perform his role without an entrepreneur), the partnership of entrepreneurial management and venture investors enables a developing business to achieve objectives faster and more efficiently. In today's dynamic and competitive marketplace such an investor/management partnership is often critical to the survival and ultimate success of new business development.

The nature of the entrepreneur/venture capitalist relationship gains even greater significance when it is compared to the relationship between venture developments and the major segments of the U.S. capital marketplace. The public stock market—with total securities valued in excess of $2 trillion—supplied at its peak activity in 1969 only $1.4 billion to small businesses and this declined to a pitiful $16 million in 1974 and 1975. In the booming new issue market of 1980, only $800 million was supplied to small business. The nation's dominant financial institutions are also not a significant factor in providing capital for venture developments. For example, the more than 14,000 commercial banks—with total assets in excess of $1 trillion—are typically risk adverse and credit oriented even in their small business loan departments. Life insurance companies and pension funds—with total assets of more than $300 billion and $600 billion, respectively—seldom make direct small business investments. In comparison, we estimate that although at the end of 1980 only $4.5 billion had been committed to venture capital investments to be made over the next five to seven years, in 1979 and 1980 this minor segment of the nation's capital resources disbursed some $1 billion each year to smaller businesses.

Because the size of the nation's total capital pool dedicated to venture capital investment is grievously small, the effective matching of entrepreneurs with venture capitalists is a very important process. This book is designed to assist in the complex matching of the entrepreneurial operating management's requirements with the objectives of the venture capitalist.

As editor of *How to Raise Venture Capital,* I wish to express thanks and appreciation to the contributing authors and to our staff members, who worked so diligently to achieve its publication.

Stanley E. Pratt

Introduction

How to Raise Venture Capital is designed to serve as a tool to assist entrepreneurs and managers in understanding how the process of raising capital actually works. Current information on the venture capital investment process and timely advice to entrepreneurs and smaller business managers who seek capital for business development are provided in articles written by professional venture investors. In these unique expositions, venture capitalists discuss their views on the key aspects of business development and clearly describe the requisite standards for their investment activities.

    The text of this book is divided into five sections relevant to the new business development process: 1) *Background*; 2) *Sources of Business Development Financing*; 3) *How to Raise Venture Capital*; 4) *When and How to Go Public*; and 5) *Perspectives*.

    Prospective entrepreneurs should find the background section quite helpful in penetrating the mystique that sometimes surrounds the venture investment process. Not only is the nature of venture capitalist involvement described, but the characteristics of successful entrepreneurs are also delineated.

2/ Introduction

Sources of business development financing are found in both the private and public sectors. Among the private venture capital sources discussed in this book are: private partnerships and corporations, publicly held venture firms, venture capital funds formed by banks and bank holding companies, divisions of major corporations, affiliates of investment banking firms, and direct venture investment activity by insurance companies, pension funds, or investment advisory firms. Several sources of government funding are reviewed in this book, including Small Business Investment Companies (SBICs) and Minority Enterprise Small Business Investment Companies (MESBICs), which are privately capitalized venture capital firms, licensed and regulated by the Small Business Administration. They are eligible to receive federal loans to leverage and augment the private funds invested in them. Both SBICs and MESBICs are privately managed and are operated in much the same manner as other venture firms. MESBICs are chartered to make equity investments in businesses owned by minority groups such as blacks, American Indians, and U.S. military Vietnam veterans. Government funding provided by Community Development Corporations and Economic Development Commissions are also discussed.

Raising venture capital can be a traumatic experience for the uninitiated, yet if one is aware of the expectations of the venture capitalists, much of the frustration and wasted energy can be alleviated. The articles in the section *How to Raise Venture Capital* are written by professional venture capitalists who seek to do just that—save their own time and energy, as well as that of the entrepreneur, by clearly laying out realistic expectations and normal procedures for approaching a venture capitalist.

While the primary thrust of this book is to obtain financing from private venture capital firms, we have included a section on *When and How to Go Public*. Not all businesses are able to attract private financing and the public marketplace is a viable alternative that has nurtured many successful developments. The differences between private and public financing of venture developments are significant. Private venture capitalists may be defined as "participating investors seeking to add value through ongoing longer-term oriented involvement with a continuing business development." As such, they are concerned investors and, in contrast to passive investors, will accept responsibility for better or for worse. Public investors, however, are passive investors and when problems develop—as they always do—the liquidity of a public market investment enables investors to walk away from one situation in search of another. Doing business in the goldfish bowl of the public market, operating managements have additional, unsophisticated pressures for performance, and each misstep is clearly exposed. A normal progression of business development financing would entail private investment until such time as a business success was clearly evident, and its profitability had provided a margin for error to overcome subsequent problems.

Understanding the different viewpoints involved in the venture development process increases the chances of establishing a productive, working relationship with a venture capitalist. Such a relationship has many times proven to be the critical element that determines a venture's success or failure. The information in the *Perspectives* section provides an insight into the personal characteristics that venture capitalists look for in their clients, as well as a view of the venture process from an entrepreneur's perspective.

Venture capital financing is primarily regarded as the early-stage financing of relatively small, rapidly growing companies. Since the recession of 1974, however, venture capitalists have taken on an expanded role in business development financing. Today, their investment activity covers a broad spectrum of investment interests encompassing virtually all phases of business development. Venture capitalists provide early-stage development funding and expansion financing for companies that have overcome initial hurdles and require additional capital for growth but do not yet have access to public or credit-oriented institutional funding. In addition, venture capitalists, together with entrepreneurs and business managements, finance management/leveraged buyouts to purchase major corporate divisions or absentee-owned private businesses, with the objective of revitalizing an existing business.

Definitions for the stages of business development funding referred to in this book are given below:

EARLY-STAGE FINANCING

- *Seed Financing*—a relatively small amount of capital provided to an investor or entrepreneur to prove a concept. It may in-

4/ Introduction

volve product development but rarely involves initial marketing.

- *Startup*—financing provided to companies for use in product development and initial marketing. Companies may be in the process of being organized or they may have been in business a short time (one year or less), but have not sold their product commercially. Usually, such firms would have assembled the key management, prepared a business plan, made market studies, and generally prepared themselves to do business.
- *First-Stage Financing*—financing provided to companies that have expended their initial capital (often in developing a prototype), and require funds to initiate commercial manufacturing and sales.

EXPANSION FINANCING

- *Second-Stage Financing*—working capital for the initial expansion of a company which is producing and shipping, and has growing accounts receivable and inventories. Although the company has clearly made progress, it may not yet be showing a profit.
- *Third-Stage Financing*—funds provided for major expansion of a company whose sales volume is increasing, and that is breaking even or profitable. These funds are utilized for further plant expansion, marketing, working capital, or development of an improved product.
- *Fourth-Stage Financing*—financing for a company expecting to go public within six months to a year. Often bridge financing is structured so that it can be repaid from the proceeds of a public underwriting. It can also involve restructuring of major stockholder positions through secondary transactions. Restructuring positions would be undertaken if there were early investors who wanted to reduce or liquidate their positions, or if management had changed and the stockholdings of the former management, their relatives, and associates were to be bought out to relieve a potential overhead stock supply when public.

ACQUISITION/MANAGEMENT BUYOUT FINANCING

- *Acquisition Financing*—funds provided to a firm to finance its acquisition of another company.
- *Management/Leveraged Buyout*—funds provided to enable operating management to acquire a product line or business (which may be at any stage of development), from either a public or private company; often these companies are closely held or family owned. Management/leveraged buyouts usually involve revitalizing an operation, with entrepreneurial management acquiring a significant equity interest.

Deciding which method or what venture capital firm or type of firm is best suited to handle a specific situation is an issue that must be resolved by the company seeking financing and by its advisors. Each venture capital firm has its own preferences, methods of investigating and selecting investments, and its own type of legal investment agreements. Since no two venture firms operate in exactly the same way, it is essential that entrepreneurs and business managers analyze their own needs and attempt to match those requirements with the skills and interests of an appropriate venture capital firm.

While most venture capital firms are devoted primarily to venture financing, there is no assurance that at any given time a specific group will be receptive to new investments or have funds immediately available. At the present time, however, most venture capitalists are relatively liquid and are actively seeking new investment opportunities. Even with the current availability of investment capital, we should point out that the majority of new investment proposals are not financed. Convincing venture capitalists that a potential development represents a unique opportunity truly represents the first major sale of a new business development. Further, a good working partner relationship must be established and maintained for the optimum benefits of venture capital investment.

Different firms have different capacities for servicing client companies and it is critical for the entrepreneur or business management to understand those capabilities. Some firms can provide a wide range of financial and managerial services, while others may have specialized talents that would be valuable to some new business developments but relatively unimportant to other specific situations. The active involvement of venture capitalists does vary in both nature and extent. Generally the most successful venturers are actively involved in the companies they finance. It is incumbent upon the entrepreneur and management team to develop a means of evaluating the ongoing role of the venture investor.

The unique character of the venture capital industry demands special qualifications to develop a truly useful guide for dealing with the industry. For over 20 years, Capital Publishing Corporation of Wellesley Hills, Massachusetts, has been publishing *Venture Capital Journal*—the principal source of current information on venture investing. Venture Economics, a division of Capital Publishing Corporation, provides information services and research regarding the venture capital investment process. The company maintains a computerized data base of information on more than four hundred venture capital firms in the United States, including their investment preferences, particular areas of expertise and specialization, and their past investment activities. This data base is used to provide focus for entrepreneurs seeking financing for their ventures. In addition, seminars for investors, entrepreneurs, and major corporations are periodically sponsored by Capital Publishing Corporation.

The venture capital industry is growing rapidly. We are confident, however, that *How to Raise Venture Capital* is the most authoritative source of information on the venture capital industry. We feel certain that this book will be of great assistance to entrepreneurs, managers of smaller businesses, and potential participants in the venturing process. We wish all of you much success with your endeavors.

BACKGROUND

Venture capital, traditionally a low-profile, private industry, is not very well understood by a majority of its potential users. One of the main objectives of this book is to replace misconceptions with a clear picture of the hard realities of venture capital financing. The first article in this section, "Overview and Introduction to the Venture Capital Industry," offers a background to enable greater understanding of the business development financing process. It examines those factors that define the industry—the long-term nature of investments and the "value added" to a new business by ongoing involvement of professional venture capitalists—and it reviews the industry's development and evolution from its original orientation towards early-stage investments to the present activity which encompasses all stages of business development.

The unique qualities of entrepreneurs are examined in "Characteristics of a Successful Entrepreneur." Written by three professionals who specialize in assessing the personal qualifications of potential entrepreneurs, this article outlines the characteristics most necessary to undertake new venture development. Also included are criteria that can be used to judge a new venture's viability, its potential, and its major risks.

Understanding the operations of the venture capital industry and the process of new business development, as well as the individual roles involved, is of critical importance to the potential entrepreneur. The following two articles begin to build that understanding.

Overview and Introduction to the Venture Capital Industry

STANLEY E. PRATT

WHAT IS VENTURE CAPITAL?

Venture capital is often thought of as "the early-stage financing of relatively small, rapidly growing companies." Although historically this has been the main thrust of venture capital, and it remains so, venture capital investment today covers a relatively broad spectrum of interests. Venture capitalists provide seed, startup, early-stage development, and rounds of expansion financing to companies that have already demonstrated the viability of their business but do not yet have access to public or credit-oriented institutional funding. They also provide management/leveraged buyout financing to assist operating managements in purchasing and revitalizing a division of a major corporation or an absentee-owned private business. Venture capitalists are even employing their skills and experience in public stock market securities, where patient, supportive investment can assist ongoing business development.

Given this range of activities, a narrow definition of venture capital is too limiting. While the close relationship between venture capitalists and entrepreneurial management teams differentiates venture capitalists from the broad world of passive investors, three additional characteristics of venture capital must be stressed:

- the potential equity participation of the venture capitalist either via a direct purchase of stock or through warrants, options, or convertible securities;
- a long-term investment discipline that requires the venture capitalist to usually wait five to ten years for investments to provide a significant return; and
- an active, ongoing involvement by the venture capitalist who brings personal value added to the capital investment.

HISTORY OF THE VENTURE CAPITAL INDUSTRY

While venture capital was instrumental in the discovery of America —remember Queen Isabella's backing of Columbus?—and in its development—from the trading and trapping companies to Pierre DuPont's investment in General Motors—its institutionalization as an industry did not start until after World War II. Prior to that time, most venture investment activity was conducted by wealthy individuals, syndicates organized by investment bankers, or by a few family organizations employing professional managers. Several of these pioneering venture firms such as Bessemer Securities, Venrock Associates (formerly Rockefeller Brothers, Inc.) and J. H. Whitney & Co. continue to be active today.

The formation of Boston's American Research and Development Corporation (ARD) in 1946 was the first step towards the institutionalization of the venture investment process. The next major milestone in the industry's development was the enactment of the Small Business Investment Act of 1958. That act provided for the creation of Small Business Investment Companies (SBICs) as vehicles for small business financing. With tax advantages and potential Government lending for leverage, SBICs were the first vestige of a true venture capital industry—and almost the last.

Although initial acceptance was slow, the SBIC program soon took off and from 1960 through 1962 approximately 585 SBIC

Overview and Introduction to the Venture Capital Industry / 11

licenses were approved. The industry was off on a fast track, but pulled up lame almost immediately. Unreasonable expectations, inadequate private capitalization, a short-term investment orientation, excessive government regulation, poor economic and market conditions, a lack of experience, and widespread misunderstanding of venture investment disciplines almost destroyed the infant industry.

SBICs were, however, a major factor in building a venture capital industry, and today the survivors form an important core of the business development investment community. Largely because of the early SBIC failure to fully take advantage of an attractive segment of the investment market, a number of new private venture capital firms were formed in the late 1960s and early 1970s.

These new firms were structured to avoid many of the problems evident in the SBIC program, such as constricting governmental regulations and inadequate private capitalization. While most new firms were formed as limited partnerships, a number of the largest firms were structured as corporations. The principal funding came from institutional and sophisticated investors such as insurance companies, pension funds, endowments, and bank trust departments, as well as wealthy individuals and families. These investors sought exceptional rewards from "high risk" venture investments. By this time the success of ARD and its investment in Digital Equipment Corporation had become visible, and new capital was attracted by the potential benefits of venture investing under disciplined management. Raising some $450 million from 1969 to 1973, new groups became active business development investors, and soon experienced some of the inherent difficulties in long-term private investment.

Many of the new venture groups initially made classic early-stage business development investments, and as a result they experienced a myriad of difficulties before some of these early-stage investments began to emerge as viable businesses. With the losing investments becoming evident early and the ultimately successful business experiencing nerve-wrenching growing pains, the feasibility of venture capital as a reasonable investment strategy was questioned by many of the institutional investors. Even sophisticated and supposedly long-term investors found it difficult to believe that the sun would eventually shine on the apparent chaos of venture investment portfolios. In addition, portfolio companies starting to achieve success were stung by the recession of 1974 and 1975. However, by the late 1970s as the venture capital partnerships began to mature, it became apparent that investment returns would far exceed those of alternative investment vehicles.

Of even greater significance than these initial investment returns were the many lessons learned and the disciplines adopted by both venture capitalists and their investors as the industry evolved during difficult economic times.

Perhaps the most important skill developed by venture capitalists during this formative period was the capability to work with operating managements over an extended period of time. The illiquidity of investment positions forced the venture investors to become involved on a continuing basis and thereby demonstrated the powerful value added effect of personal involvement in long-term investments.

In addition, adverse economic pressures resulted in the emergence of two new strategies—wider investment interests and greater industry cooperation—which strengthened the industry and filled a widening gap in financing the nation's small businesses. Although venture capitalists initially concentrated on early-stage investments, the declining public market for new issues forced venture capitalists to become more involved in expansion financings to support the development of existing portfolio companies (small company underwritings decreased from almost $1.4 billion in 1969 to less than $20 million in 1975).

With the increased demand from capital-starved, smaller businesses, venture capitalists began to operate across a far broader spectrum of investment interests. Later-stage expansion financings for companies that would have formerly received growth capital from public market underwritings provided adequate investment returns at a far lower risk exposure than early-stage developments. Startup activity was focused principally on the most qualified managements with achievable expectations. Developing these exceptional opportunities gave venture investors an insight into the requisite parameters for successfully developing new businesses. Well-structured, management/leveraged buyouts provided excellent returns with less need for continuing involvement. In 1974 venture capitalists perceived opportunities in the depressed stock market and many found—with their longer-term outlook, concerned involvement, and understanding of emerging growth company development—the public marketplace provided another area of opportunity.

This diversity of opportunities enabled venture capitalists to balance their activities in terms of time involvement, risk acceptance, and reward potential, while providing ongoing assistance to developing businesses. Some firms tailored their operations to those specific segments of the venture investment process where their particular skills would be most effective, while others developed the capability to operate across the entire spectrum of investment opportunities.

THE VENTURE CAPITAL INDUSTRY TODAY

Although there is now a smaller number of active industry participants than at the beginning of the last decade, the surviving core is experienced in venture investment disciplines and is well capitalized. A dramatic expansion of the venture capital industry began in 1978 under the impetus of the 1978 capital gains tax reduction and is continuing today. With an estimated $4.5 billion in committed capital, the industry has at least 50% more resources than it did only three or four years ago. In addition to the recent expansion of the organized venture capital industry with its professional managers, there has been a resurgence of virtually all aspects of business development investment in 1980. A blend of classic startup and early-stage investors, generalists providing expansion financing, and specialists for specific industries as well as for management/leveraged buyouts, now makes venture capitalists an attractive source of financing for more entrepreneurs and managers than ever before. In 1979 and 1980 venture capitalists disbursed an estimated $1 billion each year across the entire spectrum of their investment interests—more than double the average annual disbursements of the prior five years.

As a classic example of greater supply producing greater demand, the entire business development process has become healthy and vibrant. Non-professional individual investors in venture developments have reemerged, apparently overcoming the strong risk aversion produced by the recession of 1974 and 1975. Even the public marketplace is once again financing smaller businesses as demonstrated by a dramatic increase in underwritings of companies with a net worth of $5 million or less.

Perhaps the most remarkable social development of the late 1970s, however, was the reemergence of entrepreneuriship in the nation. Colleges today are bursting with young entrepreneurs driven by the apparent availability of funds, and they are creating more opportunities than ever before as each successful funding stimulates other attempts.

Governmental attitudes towards venture capital are now far more favorable than in the past due to the increased visibility of the broad productivity benefits of venture capital investment. With the obvious success of the 1978 capital gains tax reduction, and the Reagan administration's commitment to "supply-side economics," further incentives and legislation favorable to the venture capital industry are expected from both Congress and the administration.

The venture capital industry should maintain and build upon its present momentum in the 1980s because of the exciting synergy produced by the cooperation and coordination of capital sources, venture development investors, and entrepreneurial managers. This nation's future growth and productivity can be dramatically enhanced by a more effective utilization of these available resources.

Characteristics of a Successful Entrepreneur

ALEXANDER L. M. DINGEE, JR.,
LEONARD E. SMOLLEN,
and BRIAN HASLETT

What are the personal characteristics required to be a successful entrepreneur? Before making the great personal sacrifices required to start and build a major enterprise, potential entrepreneurs should engage in serious soul searching to be sure they have the capabilities to thrive in perhaps the toughest jungle of the business world.

To assist in such self-judgments, the following guidelines have been prepared by principals of Venture Founders Corporation (VFC), which was founded in 1970 to develop and test new approaches to venture development and investments. VFC presently serves investor clients in the United States, Canada, and the United Kingdom. These clients are committing funds to new and young ventures that are found and evaluated by Venture Founders Corporation.

Venture capitalists say that they prefer to look at a grade A manager with a grade B business idea than a grade B manager with a grade A idea. And it is often strong management teams rather than lone entrepreneurs that they end up financing.

So, the first two questions a would-be entrepreneur must ask himself are, Do I have adequate *commitment, motivation,* and *skills* to start and build a major business—to be a successful entrepreneur? Does my management team have the necessary complementary skills to enable us to succeed?

If these two questions can be answered affirmatively, then a third question must be answered before it is wise to try to develop a comprehensive business plan and mount a search for venture capital: Do I have a viable venture idea?

This article will consider these three vital questions (or major risks), with most emphasis placed on the first, and most important, one.

AM I AN ENTREPRENEUR?

One way to answer this question is to compare yourself to a successful entrepreneur in a thorough and objective manner. Begin the comparison by studying the key characteristics that successful entrepreneurs, venture capitalists, and behavioral scientists say are important for entrepreneurial success.

Drive and energy level: Success as an entrepreneur demands the ability to work long hours for sustained periods with less than the normal amount of sleep.

Self-confidence: You need self-confidence—a belief in yourself and your ability to achieve your goals and a sense that events in your life are self-determined.

Long-term involvement: You have to be able to commit yourself to projects that will see completion in five to seven years and to work toward goals that may be quite distant in the future. This ability implies a total immersion and concentration on the attainment of these distant goals.

Using money as a performance measure: Money, in the form of salary, profits, or capital gains, should be viewed as a measure of what you are doing and have done, not as an end in itself.

Persistent problem solving: You must have an intense and determined desire to complete a task or solve a problem.

Setting challenging but realistic goals: You need the ability to set clear goals and objectives that are challenging, yet realistic and attainable.

Taking moderate risks: Entrepreneurial success implies a preference for taking moderate, calculated risks, where the chances of winning are not so small as to make the effort a gamble, nor so large as to make it a sure thing, but which provide a reasonable and challenging chance of success.

Learning from failure: You have to use failures as learning experiences, and you need to understand your role in causing failures so that you can avoid similar problems in the future. You should be disappointed but not discouraged by failure.

Using criticism: You need the demonstrated capacity to seek and use criticism of your performance so that you can take corrective action and do better next time.

Taking initiative and seeking personal responsibility: You need the desire to seek and take initiative and to put yourself in situations where you are personally responsible for the success or failure of the operation. You should be able to take the initiative to solve problems or fill leadership vacuums, and you should enjoy being involved in situations in which your impact on a problem can be measured.

Making good use of resources: Can you identify and use expertise and assistance that is relevant to the accomplishment of your goals? You can't be so involved in the achievement of your goals and in independent accomplishment that you will not let anyone help you.

Competing against self-imposed standards: Do you tend to establish your own standard of performance, which is high yet realistic, and then compete with yourself?

No one individual is likely to be exceptionally strong or weak in all of these 12 attributes, and weak spots often can be covered by other members of your management team. Remember, though, *you* are the *most* critical risk. Rate yourself "strong," "average," or "weak" on each of these key characteristics compared with others you know in business. Be as honest and accurate as you can. If you think you are average or low on most of them, do yourself, your family, and your would-be backers, partners, and employees a favor—don't start a business.

If you rate yourself high on most traits, we urge you to review your ratings of yourself with people whom you respect. Wives, teachers, workmates, peers, and professional advisors are all likely to have a somewhat different view of you, in terms of both your past accomplishments and your potential. Take enough time with each reviewer to explain *why* you rate yourself as you do. Be prepared to alter your ratings in the light of their opinions. If people you know think that you will fail as an entrepreneur, they may well be right. But both you and they should be aware that making such an evaluation realistically is no quick and easy task.

Once you believe that you have a fairly good assessment of yourself, be on the lookout for personal experiences that call for entrepreneurial strengths. Reflect on these experiences and see if you behaved in a manner consistent with your rating. Self-deception is a dangerous enemy in this process of self-evaluation.

If, after a while, you can convince yourself and others you consult that you have enough entrepreneurial traits to start and build a major business, you still have to evaluate your management skills. If you lack some of the skills needed in your venture, they can be provided by others on your management team—but only if you are aware of your personal shortcomings and perceive the need for such skills. To this end, you should systematically audit your managerial experience and accomplishments in the functions of marketing and sales; operations; research, development, and engineering; financial management; general management and administration; personnel; and the legal and tax aspects of the business. To rate yourself, we suggest the following standards.

Strong = Know thoroughly and have proven ability
Average = Have limited knowledge and accomplishments and need backup
Weak = Unfamiliar and have no proven ability

Individuals are rarely equally strong in all elements of any of these seven functions. It is unwise to generalize about anyone's ability to perform an entire function from his strength in one or two of its elements. The different nature of each element makes this unlikely. For example, a powerful direct salesman probably will not show equal strength in market research and evaluation.

Before giving yourself an overall rating on each of these functions, we suggest that you break each function into its principal elements and rate yourself on each element. Note that the specific elements of any function may vary somewhat with each venture: The marketing and sales function, for example, could include market research and evaluation, marketing planning, sales management and merchandising, direct selling, service, and distribution. A listing and brief description of representative elements of all seven functions is presented at the end of this article.

We suggest that you review the self-evaluation of your management skills with people who are most exposed to them on a day-to-day basis, that is, those with whom you work or have worked. Bear in mind that bosses, peers, and subordinates may all see a different side of you. When, with the help of friends and colleagues, you have made a thorough evaluation of your entrepreneurial traits and your management skills, you should be better able to evaluate the personal risks you will run if you try to create a business.

If your dream is to build a multi-million dollar business, you might also check your evaluation with one or more of the professionals who are active and respected in the fields of career counseling and entrepreneurial behavior. A man with a weak heart may only ask his wife about taking a gentle stroll up a small grassy hill, but it would be wise to consult a doctor before he tries climbing a rocky mountainside.[1]

DOES MY TEAM HAVE THE NECESSARY COMPLEMENTARY SKILLS?

Research into successful ventures shows that teams perform better than one individual. Knowing this, venture capitalists always look for a balanced team. So your next task is to analyze the business you contemplate and determine what abilities and skills are critical to its success in the first one or two years. Then you should set about building a management team that includes people who are strong where you are weak.

In a new company, you will not want (and cannot afford) all functions performed by full-timers. You should, however, be just as careful in choosing part-timers, since you may want some of them to come on board later. Avoid the trap of teaming up with a

---

[1] For a discussion and appraisal of such evaluations, see "Business Leadership Training: A Six-Month Evaluation," a paper by Jeffry A. Timmons, D.B.A. professor, Northeastern University, and associate of Venture Founders Corporation; and John L. Hayes, Venture Founders Corporation.

school friend whom you only know in social and classroom situations or a colleague in the labor office whose skills match your own. It is tempting to do this because you think you know them, but such choices rarely work out well. Successful venture capitalists are rapidly turned off by a team that is all one of a kind—be they all engineers, salesmen, or relatives.[2]

DO I HAVE A VIABLE IDEA?

Imagine that you are sitting in a venture capitalist's chair and you have just analyzed what you did with the few hundred business proposals you examined last year. Your analysis shows that you handled the various proposals in these ways.

1. Rejected most of them after a 20 to 30 minute scanning.
2. Reviewed many others for up to two hours and then discarded them.
3. Investigated quite a few in depth and then refused them because of one or more serious flaws in the management team or the business plan—flaws that could not be remedied.
4. Investigated only a few in depth and decided to invest, but then could not negotiate acceptable terms with the entrepreneur(s) and other existing stockholders.
5. Investigated the remaining few in depth and decided to invest, then negotiated favorable terms and invested.

The 10% that you investigated in depth were presented by strong, well-balanced management teams who had been able to show you relevant accomplishments in marketing, finance, and operations. The 3% in which you had wanted to invest had developed (perhaps with some prodding by you) a comprehensive business plan.

Now, return to your real role—that of an entrepreneur. Think about what the venture capitalist's analysis means to you: You have a 3-in-100 chance of securing capital to invest, on terms acceptable to you and the venture capitalist; you have only a 1-in-

---

[2] For further discussion, see "The Entrepreneurial Team: Formation and Development" by Jeffry A. Timmons, D.B.A., a competitive paper presented at the annual Academy of Management meeting in 1973.

10 chance of being considered seriously for investment by the venture capitalist; and you must have a comprehensive business plan to be considered seriously.

You can approach several venture capitalists to find those with different standards. However, their standards will not differ widely. So, if you are really serious about going into business for yourself, you *must* start to develop a comprehensive business plan. Remember, though, if the plan is done properly and completely, it will probably take you 150 to 300 hours of hard work. Even when it is done, there is no guarantee that you will raise enough investment capital.

Is there any way to avoid having your plan rejected after a mere 20-minute scanning? Try looking at your business startup idea in the same way the venture capitalist will—in a cold, critical, unemotional manner.

Before writing your business plan, ask yourself the simple but vital questions that the venture capitalist has in his mind when he is scanning a plan to determine if it is worth studying and calling a meeting to discuss. The first vital question: *What* exactly will be sold and *to whom?* Other key market questions are:

- Why will the customer buy *your* product?
- Who are its ultimate users and what major influences on their purchasing habits are beyond your control?
- Who will be your competitors? Are they profitable now? Why do you think you can successfully compete with them?
- Is your market large and growing? Does it offer a multi-million dollar potential for you?
- Are you or will you be in a recognized growth industry?

You should then ask and answer several questions about the other major aspects of the business you contemplate, that is, questions about operations and finance. Such questions may include:

- How many dollars and months will be needed before your product is ready for market?
- What is the depth of your team's knowledge and extent of their track records in the markets, technologies, and types of operations in which you will be active?
- What are your team's management skills in the three *key* areas of marketing, finance, and operations?

- How many unproven technical, manufacturing, and marketing approaches do you contemplate?
- What are the strengths, weaknesses, and major risks of your venture?

Careful thought about the key areas listed should enable users of this guide to take a reasonable first look at their own venture ideas and to evaluate their potential and their major risks. If you are comfortable with your own answers in all of the areas discussed, you can probably justify developing a business plan. See the article, "Preparing A Business Plan," in this guide for an outline for doing this in a fashion most likely to attract and convince a professional venture capital investor. If you are uneasy in any area, is this because you lack data? Or does your venture have a basic flaw?

IN SUMMARY

The risks in entrepreneurship are you, your team, and any fundamental flaws in your venture idea. You must make a reasonable first evaluation of these risks. You should then be able to put together a business plan and avoid many of the early errors (for example, team inadequacies and problems) that so often cripple new ventures. You should also be able to improve your chances of securing financing and launching a successful venture.

REPRESENTATIVE ELEMENTS OF SEVEN MANAGEMENT FUNCTIONS

1. Marketing and sales
   a. *Market research and evaluation:* Ability to design and conduct market research studies and to analyze and interpret study results; familiarity with questionnaire design and sampling techniques
   b. *Marketing planning:* Experience in planning overall sales, advertising, and promotion programs and in deciding on and setting up effective distributor or sales representative systems
   c. *Sales management and merchandising:* Ability to organize,

supervise, motivate, and provide merchandising support to a direct sales force; ability to analyze territory and account sales potential and to manage a sales force to obtain target share of market
   d. *Direct selling:* Experience in identifying, meeting, and developing new customers; demonstrated success in closing sales
   e. *Service:* Ability to perceive service needs of particular products; experience in determining service and spare parts requirements, handling customer complaints, and managing a service organization
   f. *Distribution management:* Ability to organize and manage the flow of the product from manufacturing through distribution channels to the ultimate customer, including familiarity with shipping costs, scheduling techniques, carriers, etc.
   g. *Overall marketing skills:* Give yourself a combined rating reflecting your skill level across all of the above marketing areas
2. Operations
   a. *Manufacturing management:* Knowledge of the production processes, machines, manpower, and space required to produce the product; experience in managing production to produce products within time, cost, and quality constraints
   b. *Inventory control:* Familiarity with techniques of controlling in-process and finished goods inventories of materials
   c. *Quality control:* Ability to set up inspection systems and standards for effective control of quality in incoming, in-process, and finished materials
   d. *Purchasing:* Ability to identify appropriate sources of supply, negotiate supplier contracts, and manage incoming flow of material into inventory; familiarity with economical order quantities and discount advantages
   e. *Overall operations skills:* Give yourself a combined rating reflecting your skill level across all of the above operations areas
3. Research, development, and engineering
   a. *Direction and management of applied research:* Ability to distinguish and keep a prudent balance between long-

range projects at the frontiers of your technology, which attract the most creative individuals, and shorter-range research in support of current product development activity
    b. *Management of development:* Ability to plan and direct work of development engineers and to use time and cost budgets so that perfectionists do not ruin you and yet product performance, appearance, and production engineering needs can be met; ability to distinguish between bread-board, field, and preproduction prototype programs
    c. *Management of engineering:* Ability to plan and direct engineers in the final design of a new product for manufacture and in the engineering and testing of the production process to manufacture that new product
    d. *Technical know-how:* Ability to contribute personally to research, development, and/or engineering because of up-to-date in-depth knowledge of the technologies in which your company is involved
    e. *Overall research, development, and engineering skills:* Give yourself a combined rating reflecting your skill level across the above areas
4. Financial management
    a. *Raising capital:* Ability to decide how best to acquire funds for startup and growth; ability to forecast the need for funds and to prepare budgets; familiarity with sources and vehicles of short- and long-term financing
    b. *Money management:* Ability to design, install, maintain, and use financial controls; familiarity with accounting and control systems needed to manage; ability to set up a project cost control system, prepare cash flow and break-even analyses, analyze overhead/contribution/absorption, prepare profit and loss and balance sheets, and manage a bookkeeper
    c. *Specific skills:* Cash flow analysis; break-even analysis; contribution analysis; budgeting and profit-planning techniques; profit and loss, balance sheet, and present value analysis of return on investment and payback
    d. *Overall financial skills:* Give yourself a combined rating reflecting your skill level across all of the above financial areas

Characteristics of a Successful Entrepreneur /25

5. General management and administration
   a. *Problem solving:* Ability to anticipate potential problems and plan to avoid them; ability to gather facts about problems, analyze them for *real* causes, and plan effective action to solve the problems; thoroughness in dealing with the details of particular problems and in follow-through
   b. *Communications:* Ability to communicate effectively and clearly, both in speech and in writing, to the media, the public, customers, peers, and subordinates
   c. *Planning:* Ability to set realistic and attainable goals, identify obstacles to achieving the goals, and develop detailed action plans to achieve those goals; ability to schedule own time very systematically
   d. *Decision making:* Ability to make decisions on your best analysis of incomplete data
   e. *Project management:* Skill in organizing project teams, setting project goals, defining project tasks, and monitoring task completion in the face of problems and cost/quality constraints
   f. *Negotiating:* Ability to work effectively in a negotiating situation; ability to quickly balance value given and value received
   g. *Personnel administration:* Ability to set up payroll, hiring, compensation, and training functions
   h. *Overall administrative skills:* Give yourself a combined rating reflecting your skill level across all of the above administrative areas
6. Personnel management
   a. *Leadership:* Ability to understand the relationships between tasks, the leader, and the followers; ability to lead in situations where it is appropriate; willingness to manage actively, supervise, and control activities of others through directions, suggestions, inspiration, and other techniques
   b. *Listening:* Ability to listen to and understand without interrupting or mentally preparing your own rebuttal at the expense of hearing the message
   c. *Helping:* Ability to ask for and provide help and to determine situations where assistance is warranted
   d. *Criticism:* Ability to provide performance and interpersonal criticism to others that they find useful; ability to

receive feedback from others without becoming defensive or argumentative
- e. *Conflict resolution:* Ability to confront differences openly and to deal with them until resolution is obtained
- f. *Teamwork:* Ability to work well with others in pursuing common goals
- g. *Selecting and developing subordinates:* Ability to select and delegate responsibility to subordinates and to coach them in the development of their managerial capabilities
- h. *Climate building:* Ability to create, by the way you manage, a climate and spirit conducive to high performance; ability to press for higher performance while rewarding work well done
- i. *Overall interpersonal skills:* Give yourself a combined rating reflecting your skill level across all of the above personnel management areas

7. Legal and tax aspects
   - a. *Corporate law:* Familiarity with legal issues relating to stock issues, incorporation, distribution agreements, leases, etc.
   - b. *Contract law:* Familiarity with contract procedures and requirements (government and commercial), including default, warranty, and incentive provisions; fee structures; overhead, general and administrative expenses allowable, and so forth
   - c. *Patent law:* Experience with preparation and revision of patent applications; ability to recognize a strong patent; familiarity with claim requirements
   - d. *Tax law:* Familiarity with general state and federal reporting requirements for businesses and with special provisions concerning Subchapter S corporations, tax shelters, fringe benefits, etc.
   - e. *Overall legal tax skills:* Give yourself a combined rating reflecting your skill level across all of the above legal and tax areas

SOURCES OF BUSINESS DEVELOPMENT FINANCING

Most entrepreneurs are unaware of the myriad of financing sources available to developing businesses. This section of the book describes a variety of capital and other resources available for potential entrepreneurs.

The organized venture capital industry has widespread interests, presently has more capital available for investment than at any other time in its history, and its professional managers are actively seeking new investment opportunities in all stages of business development. Informal investors such as family, friends, and business associates are reemerging and they are a primary source of pre-startup financing. The Small Business Administration (SBA) programs including both Small Business Investment Companies (SBICs) and SBA-guaranteed loans can be an excellent source for those companies meeting the SBA's criteria. More than $3 billion has been invested by SBICs in the last 20 years. Minority Enterprise Small Business Investment Companies (MESBICs), an arm of the SBIC program, assist minority and socially disadvantaged entrepreneurs in financing their businesses. Community Development Corporations and Economic Development Commissions offer unique opportunities for companies located in specific areas or for firms willing to relocate within designated areas. In addition, venture capital subsidiaries of major corporations are becoming significant providers of independent business development financing.

This section highlights the unique characteristics of each source and presents analyses of the investment objectives as well as of the preferred type of investments and structures of these sources. This information should assist any entrepreneur in identifying those sources most apt to finance his venture.

The Organized Venture Capital Community

STANLEY E. PRATT

Peter Drucker, in his 1976 book *The Unseen Revolution: How Pension Fund Socialism Came to America,* discusses the profound changes in U.S. capital markets brought about through the growing domination of investment capital by pension funds. "We are organizing a capital market totally unequipped to supply entrepreneurial capital needs," he said, and further pointed out that "the problems of the small but growing business, while different, are also dissimilar from those of the established big or fair-sized businesses. They require a different investment policy, different relationships to management, and a different understanding of business economics, management, and dynamics." As a solution, he proffered that "what is needed, therefore, are new capital market institutions specifically provided to give these new, young, growing businesses the capital (and the management guidance) they need; and which, at the same time, can act as investment vehicles suited for the fiduciary, the asset manager trustee."

The organized venture capital community has been evolving since the 1960s to perform this role, and it now serves as an effective vehicle to distribute capital for business development invest-

30/ SOURCES OF BUSINESS DEVELOPMENT FINANCING

ment. While the total capital committed to professional venture investment management is still a small segment of the nation's vast financial marketplace, a recognized, disproportionately large benefit is accruing to this most productive segment of the American economy.

As a result of the productivity of these investments, and the current emphasis on investment versus consumption, the capital committed to professional venture capital firms is increasing. Total capital committed to this pool was approximately $2.5 to $3 billion in 1969 and remained at about that level through 1977 (additions roughly equaled withdrawals during that period). In 1978, however, with the capital gains tax reduction, a dramatic expansion commenced such that by the end of 1980 the pool totaled an estimated $4.5 billion. Annual venture capital disbursements from this pool averaged approximately $365 million per annum from 1970 through 1977, grew to $550 million in 1978, and increased dramatically to about $1 billion per annum in 1979 and 1980. During the past decade there have been approximately 400 to 600 firms involved in making business development investments, with today's active participants better capitalized and more experienced than ever before. At the end of 1980 the major components of this pool, and their relative capital commitments, were as follows:

Independent Private Venture Capital Firms	$1.8 billion
Small Business Investment Companies	1.4 billion
Venture Capital Subsidiaries of large financial institutions and industrial corporations	1.3 billion
Total	$4.5 billion

INDEPENDENT PRIVATE VENTURE CAPITAL FIRMS

The principal institutional source of venture capital is independent private venture capital firms. These include the family groups involved with venture capital investment such as the Rockefeller,

Phipps, and Whitney organizations that were the predecessors for the industry today. However, greater significance is now allotted to the professional partnerships and corporations funded by pension funds, major corporations, individuals and families, endowments and foundations, insurance companies, and foreign investors. There are at present about 100 such independent firms in the U.S. that invest principally in equity in the full range of situations from startups to relatively mature companies and management/leveraged buyouts. These funds range in capital size from $10 million to $60 million, although a few are smaller or larger. Investment activity is normally at a rate of five to ten new commitments per year with each commitment receiving from $250,000 to more than $1 million.

As the major source of classic venture development funding, independent firms adopt substantially different investment orientations. Some groups specialize in early-stage business developments such as startups and even seed financings, while others prefer expansion financings or leverage buyout transactions. Leveraged buyouts enable the operating management of a division of a larger corporation, or of a privately owned business, to purchase the existing business. Also, a number of groups now operate balanced funds which invest across the entire spectrum of business development investment interests. Most of these groups invest the major portion of their funds in high technology-related businesses, although a growing number are seeking other manufacturing, distribution, and even consumer-oriented investments. Recently there has been a trend toward service businesses, particularly computer-related software companies that are broadly enough based to hold the promise of major business development. The most critical considerations for these investors are a credible management team, an identified market niche for a product with high growth potential, and the resulting possibility of developing a major new business.

Independent venture firms are generally active investors that work in conjunction with the operating managements to develop a significant business within a five- to seven-year time frame. They are seldom passive investors, and they will provide assistance in such areas as planning, personnel development, marketing, supplier relationships, and future financing requirements. Independent venture firms also carefully monitor ongoing operations, serve as a sounding board for problem resolution, and are active participants in business development decisions.

SMALL BUSINESS INVESTMENT COMPANIES (SBICs)

Of the approximately 340 regular SBICs licensed by the Federal government, perhaps one-half are primarily oriented towards venture capital investments. The balance are principally engaged in making loans to small businesses or in making investments in specific businesses such as grocery markets or movies. Lending SBICs represent the only institutional source of long-term capital for those small businesses that may be successful but clearly lack the potential to become major businesses. SBICs usually have a minimum private equity capital of $500,000 and this may range as high as $10 million. In addition, they have access to Government loans to achieve three-to-one (for lenders) or four-to-one (for venture capital investors) leveraging of the private equity capital, thereby providing a total investment potential of four or five times the private capital. Lending SBICs often make numerous small investments, but the venture investment oriented firms normally make five to ten new commitments per year ranging from $100,000 to over $1 million for each portfolio company. Because SBICs generally borrow a portion of their investment capital and this requires servicing the interest, they usually avoid straight equity investments in early-stage companies in preference to income producing preferred stock or debt instrument investment structures.

The larger venture capital oriented SBICs, with at least $1 to $2 million in private capital, generally operate very similarly to the independent private venture capital firms. Larger SBICs operate across the broad spectrum of venture investment interests, including startups, expansion financings, and management leveraged buyouts. There is far more diversity among SBICs than among independent firms in the type of investments they will consider. The emphasis on high technology-related investments is not as great as in independent firms, and SBICs represent an excellent source of financing for businesses with more moderate growth prospects and lower potential risk.

In addition to the regular SBICs, there are now 120 Minority Enterprise Small Business Investment Companies (MESBICs) that are privately owned and managed firms. These firms are licensed to provide financing to small businesses that are at least 51% owned by socially or economically disadvantaged persons, such as members of minority groups and U.S. military Vietnam veterans. Private capital in MESBICs ranges from $300,000 to more than $4 million, and those with private capital of $500,000 or more are eligible to receive Government leverage of four to one. Most MESBICs operate in a manner very similar to SBICs and pursue the common objective of adequate investment returns, but they also possess the added expectation that social benefits will result from successful investments.

VENTURE CAPITAL SUBSIDIARIES

A number of financial corporations, most notably commercial bank holding companies, have established separate subsidiaries (often in addition to SBICs) to invest in business development situations that do not meet the parent's usual investment or loan criteria or that would not qualify under SBIC regulations. While these groups do not generally announce specific capital commitments, they are limited to 5% of the parent's capital and they range from $5 million to $100 million. Investments by these groups are most often in later-stage business developments and management/leveraged buyouts. These subsidiaries are usually managed by the group's venture investment management team and commitments to individual portfolio companies generally range from $1 million to $5 million.

Venture capital investment divisions have been formed by 30 to 40 large industrial corporations, including Exxon, General Electric, and Xerox, and they represent a substantial venture capital investment source. These typically invest in situations where the product, market, or technology is related to the parent company's operations or where the business is of interest as a diversification opportunity. This particular segment of the venture capital community showed notable growth in 1979 and 1980, and it is becoming a significant factor.

In the late 1960s and early 1970s a large number of major corporations, as well as a few insurance companies, tried investing directly in venture capital situations. Both groups contributed substantial funds to those operations, yet in most cases the efforts were misguided and the results were not fruitful. Corporations stressed the "window on technology" concept to the exclusion of developing a profitable, independent new business, and insurance investors attempted to employ their credit-oriented investment analysis techniques without recognition of the specialized skills and efforts needed for equity investment requiring ongoing involvement.

The resurgence of corporate venture investment activity, however, appears to be taking place with better planning and with recognition that such groups must be independent of normal corporate activities. Corporate groups are now employing proven venture investment disciplines, such as independent profitability and a five- to seven-year investment time frame, in the attempt to create successful venture investment divisions. In many cases the corporations are investing in, and participating with, completely independent venture capital firms. If corporations are able to maintain these disciplines, the corporate subsidiary segment of the venture capital community could become a very productive component since it already represents a very significant source of capital.

GEOGRAPHIC CONSIDERATIONS

The organized venture capital industry is concentrated in several key centers: New York City, the San Francisco Bay Area, Boston, and Chicago. Secondary centers of activity are located in Minneapolis/St. Paul, Dallas/Houston, Southern Connecticut, and Washington, D.C./Baltimore. There is also increasing activity in Southern California, the Pacific Northwest, and the Southeast. While there are venture groups in each of these areas considering a broad range of investment opportunities, New York and Chicago, as major financial centers, are leading markets for leveraged buyouts and expansion financings. The San Francisco Bay Area and

Boston are focal points of high technology, as well as financial centers, and tend to concentrate in technology-based business development investment. The San Francisco Bay Area has a relatively high proportion of startups, and Boston is a leader in expansion development financings, both early and later stage. The Minneapolis/St. Paul investment pattern includes a number of medical/health care- and computer-related ventures, whereas Dallas/Houston has become a center for energy-related ventures.

Although the geographic location of a venture capital firm is a notable consideration, its importance has somewhat diminished in recent years. Increasing cooperation among venture capital firms has led to a sharing of responsibility for local monitoring and ongoing involvement. When considering an attractive venture investment opportunity in a distant area, venture capitalists today often try to involve another group located within a 200-mile radius of the business opportunity. Thus, by sharing potential rewards and responsibilities, many venture capital firms now operate virtually coast to coast. A major stimulus to this cooperation has been the development of two major trade associations, the National Association of Small Business Investment Companies (NASBIC) and the National Venture Capital Association (NVCA).

A HEALTHY AND EXPANDING INDUSTRY

While the organized venture capital industry certainly does not represent the nation's entire venture capital investment activity, its vibrancy and prosperity set the tone for overall activity. With remarkable accomplishments evident in 1979 and 1980, the venture capital industry currently enjoys excellent health from a record amount of available investment capital, the experience of two decades of development, and an entrepreneurial climate favorable for venture development investment.

Informal Investors—When and Where to Look

WILLIAM E. WETZEL, JR.

Entrepreneurs seeking risk capital should be aware that risk capital is not a homogeneous commodity and that the risk capital markets are both diverse and dispersed. Risk capital sources range from the public new issues market, through professional venture capital funds and wealthy individuals, to local investors with a few dollars to back an acquaintance or relative. Investment objectives are equally broad. For example, risk capital investors vary dramatically in their taste for risk, ranging from investors willing to back inventors with unproven ideas to those preferring second- or third-round financing for established firms. Investors differ as well in the size of the investment they will consider, their exit horizons or level of patience for cash flow, their degree of personal involvement with a venture, their geographic and industrial preferences, their rate of return requirements, and in the substitutability of nonfinancial for financial rewards.

For many entrepreneurs seeking risk capital, informal investors represent the most appropriate source of funds, if not the only source. The term *informal investors* includes sources of risk capital other than professionally managed venture capital funds, equity-oriented Small Business Investment Companies (SBICs), other institutional investors, and the public equity markets. Informal investors tend to be financially sophisticated individuals of means, e.g., net worth in excess of $250,000 and annual income in excess of $50,000, often with previous investment or management experience in new or rapidly growing ventures.

Assuming that a venture proposal is economically sound in terms of market potential, competitive advantages, production capability, etc., and that competent management is available or can be acquired, then there are definable circumstances under which a search for risk capital from informal investors would be appropriate.

FINANCING TECHNOLOGY-BASED INVENTORS

Informal investors, in particular individuals with past experience in the formation of ventures in related fields of technology, are often the most likely source of risk capital for technology-based inventors prior to the startup of a business enterprise. Venture capital firms typically have little interest in inventors. The odds of picking a winner are slim, downside risks are close to 100%, relatively small amounts of money are involved, the costs of investment supervision and guidance are high, and the length of time between investment and potential cash recapture generally exceeds the exit horizons of venture capital firms. Informal investors may accept these risks in view of perceived non-financial benefits such as the satisfaction of business creation or the stimulation of involvement, but professional venture capitalists consider the financial risk/reward relationship to be paramount.

The successful commercialization of new technology typically depends more upon "demand pull" than upon "technology push." An individual investor with technical and managerial experience in the commercialization of related technology can bring a "sense of the market" to the work of a technology-based inventor. Personal satisfaction derived from a fresh involvement with emerging technology may also convert what would be a cost to a professional investor into a significant non-financial benefit for the right individual investor. Technology-based inventors should be aware, however, that despite the potential attractiveness of participation in new technology, the financial risks are extreme. Capital gains potential on the order of 50 to 100 times or more within five to ten years is not unreasonable and may require sale of a major share of equity to attract funds. By reducing the risk and the waiting period for investors, the longer an inventor/entrepreneur can survive on personal funds and "sweat equity," the lower will be the cost of external capital.

Increasingly, technology-based inventors and small firms can turn to public and quasi-public organizations for risk financing. These relatively recent programs have been created in recognition of the contribution of young, technology-based firms to the generation of new jobs and to the pace of technological innovation, and in recognition of the difficulty these ventures encounter in raising small amounts of very high risk seed financing. At the national level, the National Science Foundation's Small Business Innovation Research Program (SBIR) is perhaps the best known and most successful. The SBIR program was initiated in 1979 to fund high-quality research proposals on scientific or technical opportunities that could have significant public benefit if the research is successful. A second goal of the SBIR program is the conversion of funded research into technological innovation by private firms. The SBIR program is designed to increase the incentive and opportunity for small firms to undertake high-risk research that has a high potential payoff and can effectively lower the risk for follow-on investors. Other national programs with similar objectives include the National Bureau of Standards Energy Related Inventions Program, the Department of Commerce Experimental Technology Incentives Program, and the Department of Energy Appropriate Technology Grants Program.

Several New England states have created their own programs to stimulate economic growth by providing risk capital for firms with promising ideas and innovations. Examples include the Connecticut Product Development Corp., the Maine Capital Corp., and the Massachusetts Technology Development Corp.

FINANCING BUSINESS STARTUPS

Since the late 1960s, most professional venture capital firms have adopted a policy of avoiding startups, and have put their available capital into safer, more liquid investments. The National Venture Capital Association found that in the mid-1970s 143 venture capital firms were investing at the rate of about $150 million annually, with less than 10% of these funds, under $15 million, going to startup situations. Fifteen million dollars will finance perhaps 20 new ventures, equivalent to 1 corporation out of every 10,000 that are formed annually.

While the 1978 reduction in capital gains tax rates and a modest revival in the public new issues market have attracted several hundred million dollars into professional venture capital portfolios, less than 15% of these funds appear to be available for startups and then only for firms with the prospect of a public share offering or merger with a larger, established firm within five to ten years. Individual investors and groups of individuals are frequently the most likely sources of startup financing.

Providing seed capital or startup financing to an inexperienced management team can be enormously time consuming. Many of the management decisions involved in creating a new venture are unique to the startup process and will set the course of the venture through its perilous early years. Investors experienced with seed capital and startup situations can provide invaluable guidance to entrepreneurs who typically are engaged in the process for the first time. Ideally, investors in new enterprises would also be experienced in related fields of business or technology. In other words, a search for the "right" investors is part of the search for funds. The right informal investors will also be individuals who are fully aware of the risks involved and who are emotionally, as well as financially, able to bear those risks; who recognize the inevitability of unforeseen delays and other problems; who are prepared to invest additional funds if the venture succeeds and/or are realistic about the cost of additional outside risk capital; whose exit expectations are consistent with those of the founder and with the cash flow requirements of the venture; and, finally, whose role in the management of the venture is compatible with the needs of the venture and the founder.

Financially sophisticated individuals and groups of individuals are an appropriate source of startup funds under some or all of the following conditions:

a. *When the total financing required is over $50,000 but under $500,000.* The lower boundary represents the approximate limit of funds often available from an entrepreneur's personal savings and other friendly sources and is the bare minimum required to start anything but a "Mom & Pop" operation. The upper boundary represents the minimum investment typically required to interest a professional venture capital firm or equity-oriented SBIC, though they will occasionally entertain proposals involving less than $250,000.

b. *When the sales potential of the venture is between $2 million and $20 million per year within five to ten years.* Ventures with a potential volume of $20 million and up are generally necessary to provide the prospect of cash recovery through a public share offering or merger with a larger firm within the typical five- to ten-year investment cycle of a professional venture fund. Informal investors tend to exhibit longer exit horizons and can accommodate firms with slower growth rates. Young, privately held firms with sales under $20 million generate the majority of new job opportunities and are a major source of technological innovation. These "foundation" firms are often initially financed by informal investors. Entrepreneurs seeking risk capital from informal investors for new foundation firms should identify the cash recapture expectations of these investors early in their negotiations and be prepared to offer appropriate buy-back arrangements or other liquidation options as an alternative to traditional exit mechanisms.

c. *When the proposed new venture is expected to generate "psychic income" for an investor in addition to adequate financial rewards.* More than impersonal financial incentives usually influence the investment decisions of informal investors. For example, a sense of civic or social responsibility often motivates individuals of means. A wealthy citizen in a community suffering from chronic unemployment may have more than a pecuniary interest in backing a venture expected to create 50 to 100 new jobs over a period of five to ten years. Other individuals may derive "psychic income" from financing an inventor/entrepreneur involved in the commercial development of a new technology with significant social benefit, e.g., medical technology or energy-related technology. Other informal investors, in particular previously successful entrepreneurs, are often interested in investing both their funds and their experience in assisting promising new ventures get started. The rewards are partly financial and partly the satisfaction and stimulation of playing a role in the entrepreneurial process.

FINANCING GROWING, ESTABLISHED BUSINESSES

Retained earnings are the primary source of equity capital to finance the growth of both public and privately held established corporations. General Electric's retained earnings are five times its paid-in capital, Kodak's seven times, and General Motors' ten times. For privately held corporations retained earnings are generally the only source of new equity capital. For example, there are over two million incorporated businesses in the United States, but only about 12,000 (approximately one-half of one percent) enjoy sufficiently wide ownership to be considered publicly owned. The shares of about 4,000 firms are traded on an organized stock exchange. In other words, the public equity markets are not a source of capital for most corporations. In testimony before the House Subcommittee on Capital Investment and Business Opportunities during 1977 hearings into small business access to equity and venture capital, M. William Benedetto, vice-president of E. F. Hutton & Co., was quoted as follows:

> Speaking directly as an investment banker, I can tell this Committee that we are unable to provide startup capital for new enterprises. The marketplace has caused us to substantially increase our criteria for providing capital to existing businesses. In short, capital in meaningful terms is available only for medium-sized companies—those with annual after-tax earnings in excess of $2.8 million.

In a 1977 position paper, the National Association of Small Business Investment Companies cited similar criteria:

> Smaller underwriters are currently insisting that a company have a minimum of $500,000 to $1,000,000 of after-tax earnings to undertake a public offering while the larger underwriters generally look for a minimum of $2,000,000.

After-tax profits of $1 to $2 million imply sales of $20 million or more, given typical profit margins of 5% to 10%.

Only the exceptional expanding foundation firms with sales between $2 million and $20 million, can generally raise funds in the public equity markets. Professional venture capital firms concentrate on businesses with prospective growth rates high enough to propel a venture into public offering status within five to ten years, or to attract major corporate acquisition.

In the absence of alternative external equity sources, growth rates for foundation firms are constrained by the growth in internally generated equity. A firm earning a 15% return on equity and paying no dividends can grow no faster than 15% per year without distorting the debt/equity proportions of its balance sheet. Growth rates in excess of 30% per year typically are necessary to attract the interest of institutional venture investors. The troublesome firm to finance is the established foundation firm growing faster than retained earnings can support but not fast enough to attract venture capital. These troublesome but attractive growth rates tend to fall between 10% and 30% per year.

For foundation firms growing at a rate too slow to attract venture capital, private individuals are the most likely financing source. A great deal of time can be wasted talking with institutional venture capital sources about deals which they are very unlikely to do. In recognition of the growth-financing problems of foundation firms and the contribution of these firms to job creation and technological innovation, legislation introduced in the 1980 session of Congress would make risk capital investment in small firms more attractive to informal investors. For example, Senate Bill 1481 would provide tax incentives in the form of a new security called a Small Business Participating Debenture to provide a source of capital for foundation firms. Key elements of S-1481 include the following advantages of a Small Business Participating Debenture (SBPD) for an individual investor:

1. Funds invested earn a share of the profits, which is taxed at the preferential capital gains tax rate.
2. The SBPD would be similar to "Section 1244 stock" in that investors would be entitled to ordinary deductions for any losses on their investments.
3. An investment tax credit would be granted to a maximum of 5% of the amount invested.

Regardless of the outcome of S-1481 and other legislation, it is encouraging to note that the capital formation problems of small firms and private investors are receiving increased attention at all levels of government.

PROFILE OF INFORMAL INVESTORS

Any attempt to describe a "typical" informal investor is bound to result in a profile with as many exceptions as examples. In the first place, these individuals exhibit a natural tendency toward anonymity when it comes to their investment activity. The Commerce Technical Advisory Board, in its 1976 report on The Role of New Technical Enterprises in the U.S. Economy, stated, "There are no data regarding the individual and truly private sources of seed money." In the second place, the personal backgrounds and investment objectives of informal investors are so diverse that generalizations about these characteristics are, at best, only suggestive.

The importance of informal investors to the vitality of foundation firms prompted a 1978 pilot research effort by the Whittemore School of Business and Economics at the University of New Hampshire. The research undertook to test two hypotheses:

1. Informal investors, essentially individuals of means, represent a potentially significant source of risk capital for foundation firms.

2. Informal investors employ investment criteria that differ in material ways from the criteria employed by professional venture capital firms.

A comprehensive investment questionnaire was used in the research. With assistance from the Small Business Association of New England (SBANE), the New England Industrial Resources Development Program (NEIRD), and others, 48 completed questionnaires were collected. The most significant results of the survey, which was concentrated in the New England area, are summarized below:

1. Average age of respondents was 48, and over half had previous experience as entrepreneurs or investors in startup situations.
2. Average investment in any one situation was $32,000, with 10% preferring to invest over $50,000 and 10% preferring to invest under $10,000. The total potential pool of risk capital represented by respondents exceeded $1 million per year over three years.
3. Respondents, in general, were interested in participating with others in venture-type investments. Preferred partners included other financially sophisticated individuals, banks, and venture capital firms.
4. Required rates of return were lower than those typically required by professional venture capitalists, ranging from 22% per year for startups to 16% per year for investments in established, growing firms. On the average, exit horizons appeared to be longer than those required by venture capital firms.
5. Over half of the respondents indicated that they would accept a lower rate of return on investment in exchange for some form of non-monetary return. The creation of local job opportunities in an area with high unemployment was an acceptable substitute for 59% of respondents, with an average ROI reduction of approximately 2%, or nearly four percentage points. Other trade-offs were also cited.
6. Respondents had been offered approximately three venture investment opportunities per year, most of which were directed to them by friends or business associates, not from sources

such as bankers, accountants, lawyers, or investment firms. Over 60% indicated an interest in a regional service that would screen and refer risk capital investment opportunities to them.

Based in part on the results of the 1978 research, the Office of Economic Research of the U.S. Small Business Administration has sponsored an expanded investigation into the cost and availability of informal risk capital in New England. The research is being conducted by the Center for Industrial and Institutional Development at the University of New Hampshire. Results of the expanded research are scheduled for publication by late 1980.

Informal investors, essentially individuals of means and successful entrepreneurs, are a diverse and dispersed group with a preference for anonymity. Creative techniques are required to identify and reach them. Currently, inventors and entrepreneurs must find their own way through the maze of channels leading to informal risk capital. Private market makers are unable, by and large, to reap the substantially public benefits of improving the efficiency of the informal capital market. Therefore, entrepreneurs can expect to find little guidance in preparing sound investment proposals and in identifying potential individual investors, and investors themselves will continue to rely largely on random events to bring investment opportunities to their attention. Among the major objectives of the current SBA-sponsored research is an assessment of the feasibility of creating an experimental mechanism to improve the efficiency of the informal risk capital markets.

SUMMARY

Wealthy individuals, successful entrepreneurs in particular, are a significant source of risk capital for certain types of situations. These informal investors are a diverse and dispersed group about which very little is known. Situations suggesting a search for risk capital from an appropriate individual, or group of individuals, include the following:

1. Financing technology-based inventors prior to commercialization of an invention or innovation.

2. Financing business startups, especially for firms with five- to ten-year sales potential between $2 million and $20 million and requiring between $50,000 and $500,000 of risk capital.
3. Financing business startups with the prospect of providing psychic income in addition to adequate financial rewards. Examples of non-financial incentives for informal investors include the creation of jobs in a community experiencing chronic unemployment, participating in the commercialization of a socially useful new technology or innovation, and the satisfaction of playing an active role in the entrepreneurial process.
4. Financing privately held, established businesses growing too fast to finance from retained earnings but not fast enough to attract institutional venture investors. Attractive but troublesome growth rates tend to fall between 10% and 30% per year.

The search for informal risk capital under the best of circumstances can be tedious and time consuming. Entrepreneurs with sound ideas, strong management skills, and well-documented proposals may find the search productive. Financially sophisticated individuals will often undertake investments that are smaller, riskier, and less liquid than those that interest professional venture investors. Appropriate incentives are necessary to offset the costs, risks, and limited liquidity of these investments and entrepreneurs seeking informal risk capital will find it essential to carefully match their objectives with those of their financial partners.

Pre-Startup Seed Capital

WILLIAM R. CHANDLER

GENERAL OBSERVATIONS

Most new venture financings occur, at least conceptually, in three stages: seed, startup, and early growth. Seed financing is a relatively small amount of capital provided to an inventor or an entrepreneur to investigate a business concept. It may involve product development but rarely involves initial marketing. As the term *seed* denotes, this capital is used to "germinate" the entrepreneur's vision of his business and to transform it into the tangible reality to attract additional capital for continued product development and initial marketing (the startup stage).

Although the new venture team may expect to raise startup capital from professional venture capital sources, any seed financing is likely to be from non-professional sources since there are few seed-financing specialists within the venture capital community. Ninety percent of the active, professional venture capital groups seldom, if ever, make seed stage investments. Typically entrepreneurs tap informal sources (such as family, friends, or groups of private investors) to combine with whatever personal capital they have. I would guess that at least 95% of the successful seed financing must still come from these traditional sources. These informal sources base their investment decisions on their knowledge of the individual and their personal assessment of the business venture.

A professional venture capital investor is a far different kind of partner than Uncle Harry. If an entrepreneur succeeds in obtaining seed financing from a professional venture capitalist he is not only gaining a valuable partner capable of offering him wisdom and guidance during the formative stage of his company, but also a partner capable of either providing later financing or helping him find it. Venture capitalists are often prepared to put more early-stage capital at risk in order to enhance the entrepreneur's opportunity to pursue an aggressive business startegy based on grabbing a large market share.

In considering a seed stage investment, the venture capitalists recognize the likelihood that they may have to wait eight, ten, or twelve years to liquidate the investment. Most venture capitalists are working with an objective of securing liquidity within five to seven years. Seed capital often has to be invested three or four years before startup venture capital—perhaps longer. Therefore, seed capital has to be the most patient of the venture investments. If a venture capitalist is willing to expend the time and resources to develop a business from its seed stage, he must perceive a minimal risk and an outstanding opportunity for return.

Raising seed capital is the first and most important selling effort of a business' life. During the seed stage, the entrepreneur will typically assemble the key management, prepare a business plan, and make extensive market studies—all three of which are the basic tools needed to sell his company to the venture capital community for future financing. The new venture team should look at the startup financing as their first $250,000, $500,000, or $1 million sale—and I am sure in their past employment they didn't close many sales of that magnitude without a carefully prepared, first-class sales program. Such a program starts with an effort to learn what the customer has been buying in the past, why, and what his needs are in today's market. If the management team hasn't had experience with the venture capital industry they should try to build up a very clear picture of what the venture capitalist will be looking for in their financing presentation.

I recommend that a team identify those sources of startup capital they expect to approach before they raise any significant seed capital or prepare a business plan. The management team should study the existing investments of these sources, form a picture of the original state of the sources' early-stage investments, and try to develop a business plan incorporating the special characteristics of their industry.

The new venture team should then turn back to their own business and try to make a cold-blooded appraisal of the management resumes, the market characteristics and the product features they are attempting to sell. Comparing that picture to the model they have to match reveals the holes that have to be filled during the seed development stage of their venture. These needs may take the form of adding more staff, reassigning people, gathering additional market information, or establishing hardware credibility. The seed stage business plan is a critical tool to convince a venture capitalist that the business is feasible, and the plan may take as long as 9 to 15 months to prepare. It should be well-structured and thought out, yet it must be adaptable and flexible to not only adjust to changes in the developing business, but also to take into account its initial presentation to various venture capitalists whose strategies and priorities may differ. The seed stage plan should also include a realistic estimate of the amount of capital required for seed and startup financings.

If the venture team at this point decides they have the credentials to solicit a combination seed/startup financing package from one of the top venture capitalists, they should prepare their business plan and go. If they can measure up, I think they will be tapping the best source of startup capital on earth. Venture capitalists will add talents the new venture team probably does not possess, and they will drag in behind them a lot of financial credibility when the enterprise needs it most.

A few new sources of seed financing have appeared recently that can be useful in certain situations. The National Science Foundation's Innovation Grant program can be helpful to the trained scientist who needs seed money to undertake an innovative research project which carries the potential for future commercial development. On the West Coast there has also been an increase in the use of tax shelter-oriented, research and development partnerships for financing technical development programs. Many of the investors are successful technologists who understand the technologies they are investing in—but it is the tax shelter benefits that persuade them to part with their money. However, the R&D partnerships leave the entrepreneurs with the problem of finding seed capital to finance all items that cannot be expensed in the development partnership.

THE EXPERIENCE OF BAY VENTURE MANAGEMENT

Five years ago Bay Venture Management was organized as a pre-venture capital seed investor. I thought I saw an opportunity for front-end, venture capital investment financings in the range of $100,000 to $150,000, with early-stage oriented venture capitalists providing subsequent financing. I was also convinced that the American financial community was, collectively, leaving a lot of technical market opportunities lying stillborn. I thought I knew of a number of potentially attractive growth markets in which we should be investing, but in which we were not seeing many good, startup offerings. In those potentially attractive markets, I wanted Bay Venture to take the initiative in organizing, staffing, and financing startup ventures.

In 1976, I sold this investment development startegy to 14 individual investors and organized Bay Venture Management, Inc. We found out after investing an average of $100,000 in each seed venture that our projects fell far short of the quality standards needed to raise startup financing from professional venture capitalists.

The venture capitalists were investing in raw startups, but they were truly skimming the cream—in 1976 and 1977 perhaps a total of 40 to 50 such proposals were being funded a year, nationwide. Not surprisingly, I found I could not put together one of the 40 or 50 best startup ventures with an expenditure of $100,000. My seed financing strategy had run into a stone wall. The basic problem was that we were taking competent, entrepreneurially inclined people and giving them seed capital when only a market had been defined, and they were identifying all kinds of potentially attractive but unproven product concepts. Locating these product opportunities and developing functioning hardware demonstrated our venture team's competency, but we were reaching the startup stage with a business plan based on a lot of assumptions, a few bits and pieces of hardware, and a lot of blue sky stretched over it with regard to what we were going to do someday. I had worked with these people for 14 to 16 months and had confidence in them. However, they weren't attractive to disinterested venture capitalists and, as a result, Bay Venture rather quickly evolved from a seed specialist into a supplier of both seed and startup capital.

In our investment program, to date, we have been operating on the assumption that each venture must produce marketable products with a cumulative investment of less than $200,000. With those kinds of limits, the startup venture teams are not embarking on any projects requiring the development of new technologies, or even pushing the state of the art in an advanced technology. For example, some of our ventures have been based on applications where we can gain a performance edge through incorporation of the control and information processing skills of the microcomputer.

When we launch a new venture project today we know it is going to require a minimum of $300,000, and it is more likely to require $500,000 to bring it through the startup stage. We have most recently been operating with a three-stage financing plan: $50,000 of seed capital to plan the enterprise; $200,000 to develop products and to begin manufacturing and marketing operations; and a later $250,000 or so to bring the venture to economic viability.

Even with this kind of financing we find our venture projects very tightly constrained with little margin for error. We must run with too thin a startup management team, and depend too much on outside contractors. We have difficulty recruiting skilled people even when we think we can afford them because of the modest capital base. There are a number of markets in which we would like to launch a new venture, but we just don't know how to do it for $500,000.

We have experienced delays, performance shortfalls, and technical problems in every venture we have participated in thus far. We have never been close to our sales forecasts during the first year or two. People who haven't been through it cannot believe how hard it is to sell unique, new products offered by an unknown, new company. But thus far we have not suffered an outright product failure and we have not had one of the startups continue for two years after first delivery of products without reaching a sales level sufficient to support profitable operations. I don't think we have yet created a startup venture that is going to cost our investors their equity capital.

People often ask me why our investors have been willing to participate in this kind of risky, long-term investment. I usually hear something like this: "Well, I admire your investors' courage, but I can't understand taking those kind of risks. After all, only 1 out of every 10 or 15 of those kind of deals ever works out." Even a few venture capitalists seem to believe this line. It is not true.

I don't believe the risks are unacceptably high when investing in startup ventures that are based on marketing product concepts from experienced people who have a good grounding in applications engineering. If one follows our practice of only investing at the inception of the business at founders' share prices, and, as with our ventures to date, the company goes on to reach profitable operations within three or four years, that going business is probably worth several times per share what we initially paid.

Each of the businesses we have started that has reached the point of product sales, is growing at a rate exceeding 40% per annum. Taken collectively they are more than doubling their sales every one and one-half to two years. Growing and profitable technical companies are usually worth at least their annual sales totals. After allowing some dilution of ownership to acquire added equity to fund growth, the founders shares in such ventures will appreciate at an average rate of 35% to 40% per annum over a five- to ten-year period—even if one never manages to invest in that ubiquitous "next Xerox." The big successes, if any, will do better, and the failures may only yield a tax write-off, but an investor can make a very acceptable return in this business even if he is writing off one out of every three or four ventures he invests in. And I don't think any of the early-stage oriented, California-based venture capitalists are losing 25% of their investments, nor do I expect Bay Venture to suffer losses exceeding 25% even though we are investing entirely at the startup stage.

We have been telling our investor group that they should expect to see their position in each venture held eight to ten years. A little less than five years into the investment program, we are still working for growth, not liquidity.

CONCLUSION

Throughout the last decade, seed and startup capital have been extremely difficult to locate. Venture capital is now a growth industry, with more and more dollars becoming receptive to earlier stage investing. An increasing number of venture capitalists are learning to evaluate, finance and assist in the new venture development process. There is every indication that these skills can be learned and taught; and when they are assimilated they will yield venture investment managers who will beat down the historic loss experience of the industry. Who knows, with enough success, and perhaps some assistance on the regulatory and tax fronts from the Government, seed and startup stage investing may one day be recognized for what it is—the most profitable segment of the venture capital marketplace.

SBA Programs for Financing a Small Business

DAVID J. GLADSTONE

There are two basic U.S. Small Business Administration (SBA) programs that have been used most frequently to finance small business. The first program is through Small Business Investment Companies (SBICs) licensed by the SBA and second is through SBA 90% guaranteed loans from conventional lending institutions.

SBIC FINANCING

During the last two decades, the SBIC industry has developed into a unique source of funds for small business in the United States. During these past 20 years, SBICs have invested $3 billion in small businesses, with only about $30 million in losses to the Small Business Administration. SBICs have contributed to the creation of millions of jobs by their investments in small business. By any test, the SBIC program has been a success. It has been an ideal marriage between public policy and private enterprise.

Each SBIC is a private company owned by investors and has

equity capital contributed by the stockholders. During the last 20 years, there was rapid growth in the number of SBICs, a period of no growth, and then a decline. More recently, the number of SBICs has increased dramatically. Currently, there are approximately 350 active SBICs in the United States. Each must invest its funds only in U.S.-based small businesses. To receive a list of the most active SBICs, one should write to the National Association of Small Business Investment Companies, 618 Washington Building, Washington, D.C. 20005.

The most noticeable development in the SBIC industry in recent years has been the increase in the number of professional managers. Most managers have advanced business degrees and experience in the field of lending or equity financing and are therefore able to act in a knowledgeable and professional manner. Another change that a small business should be aware of is the trend of the SBIC community into a narrow spectrum of structuring SBIC investments. Since SBICs borrow most of their funds from the SBA—up to $4 in loans from the SBA for each $1 of private capital—the type of deal they can offer is limited. While most have not fully leveraged available borrowings, the constraints of this debt influence SBIC investment structuring.

As with most things in this world, the cost of SBIC borrowing has increased dramatically. Recently, SBICs were paying the SBA 12% interest for their funds. Thus, the problem in structuring an investment to a small business is that the SBIC has borrowed most of its money and, therefore, needs to charge interest on the money it disburses to the small business so it may pay the SBA for the interest on its own loans. Because of this cash flow need, SBICs most normally lend their money, rather than buy stock in a small business. Usually, they lend their money at 12%-15% interest. Most of the interest paid by the small business to the SBIC is, in turn, paid to the SBA. Any difference is used to cover operating overhead in the SBIC.

As one can see, most of the loan income from small businesses does not generate a great profit for the stockholders of the SBIC. Rather, the SBICs make their profit by having an option to own equity in the small business to which they have loaned money. The typical types of financing done by SBICs in order of their frequency are outlined as follows:

LOAN WITH OPTIONS TO BUY STOCK

A loan for eight years, three years interest only, then five-year amortization; 13% to 15% interest; usually subordinated to institutional lenders, with stock options on 10%-25% of the company's stock at a low exercise price. This is usually a third-round financing.

CONVERTIBLE DEBENTURE

A convertible debenture for ten years, five years interest only, then five years of amortization; 10%-14% interest, unsecured with conversion privileges for 25%-30% of the stock of the borrower at a reasonable price. This is usually a second-round financing.

STRAIGHT LOAN

A loan at 15%-17% interest with a straight amortization over five to seven years, secured by specific assets. This is usually financing for a mature company secured by specific assets.

PREFERRED STOCK

Preferred stock redeemable after ten years, with an 8% to 10% dividend, with an option to convert to common stock of approximately 40% to 80% of the company. This is usually first-round financing.

SBA FINANCINGS

Notice that these investments, except for the last one, are loans and not equity. Few SBICs make common stock equity investments because of their SBA interest obligations discussed above. Most analysts of the SBIC program now recognize that if the program is to be equity-oriented, the SBA is going to have to change its program and purchase preferred stock from SBICs and, in return, the SBICs will be required to purchase equity in the small business.

Even today, many small businessmen don't understand why SBICs don't want to purchase stock in their small business. On the other hand, most small businessmen will not borrow money from their bank to purchase stock in a friend's company. Obviously, SBICs have the same problem, due to the funds borrowed from the SBA. So, the best advice to a small business seeking financing from an SBIC is to structure the proposed investment as a loan with equity options, or like one of the items above. To structure the proposed financing any other way will risk a premature turndown by the SBIC.

Another angle on the types of investments SBICs make is determined by the stage of development of the corporate entity or business. A compendium, with amounts of equity required, is set forth below.

STARTUPS OR FIRST-ROUND FINANCINGS

These are the most difficult situations to finance through a SBIC because a new company needs equity and not debt since it needs to retain its cash flow in the initial years to use internally, rather than pay interest on SBIC debt. Some SBICs will, however, invest a portion of their funds in early-stage financings and approximately 20% of the funds invested by SBICs today are in new companies.

SECOND-ROUND FINANCING

Here, the company has created a product of service and is marketing it with some degree of success and needs funds to finance the business' growth. In those cases, a convertible debenture is normally the structure.

THIRD-ROUND FINANCING

When a company is running well and has generally established profitability, but needs growth capital, a loan with warrants will typically be the structure.

PUBLIC OFFERING

Sometimes, an SBIC will purchase preferred stock or a convertible debenture that is part of a public offering or a semi-public offering. In this instance, the company is usually well along in its development cycle and investment risk can be more clearly analyzed and managed.

LEVERAGE BUYOUT

In many cases a company may be purchased by new owners with mostly debt. Often the current operating management participates in the purchase. Those businesses usually have demonstrated cash flow to service such debt. SBICs often provide subordinated debt in the form of loans with warrants. The SBIC debt in fact supports senior debt since it may be unsecured or so far down the ladder from security that a senior lender really thinks of it as equity.

STRAIGHT DEBT

There are a number of SBICs that make collaterized loans for a simple high-interest rate. Usually, this is done when the SBIC has excess funds; however, there are a number of SBICs that concentrate or specialize in this type of financing.

TURN-AROUND

Some SBICs finance turn-around situations—companies in trouble (even bankruptcy) which need money and management assistance. Usually, a turn-around deal is structured as debt with equity.

As you can see, you are more likely to receive financing from an SBIC if you are seeking a second- or third-round financing. But a potential borrower from an SBIC must know the type of SBIC that may be interested in financing their concern. There are various types of SBICs with different investment objectives.

PUBLIC COMPANIES

Some of the largest SBICs are owned by public stockholders and their stock trades on the stock markets. Because of the problems of operating a venture capital company and meeting the requirements of the Investment Company Act of 1940, there are not many of these available for small business. Before their demise, many of the public companies tended to be the greatest risk takers. With a few exceptions, however, most of the remaining public SBICs are now making second- and third-round financings. Recently, the Small Business Investment Incentive Act of 1980 created "Business Development Companies" that can operate as public venture capital companies or SBICs without the major constraints of the 1940 Act, but it is too early to describe their character and structure.

PRIVATE COMPANIES

Most of the SBICs today are privately owned, which gives them great flexibility to meet the needs of the small businessmen. Since the management of the SBIC answers only to a few private stockholders, specific needs of the entrepreneur can often be discussed with the principals of the SBIC to provide the type of financing and flexibilities needed.

BANK-RELATED

Many SBICs are owned by banks. Too often, these are merely extensions of the bank loan department. In larger banks, however, the SBIC is generally a profit center with its own management team which can accommodate the small business on terms and conditions. Bank loan departments often team up with the SBIC where the bank makes a working capital loan on inventory and receivables and the SBIC makes an equity-type, long-term loan. This combination has proved to be excellent in many cases.

VENTURE CAPITAL-RELATED

Some SBICs are wholly owned subsidiaries of a pool of capital used for venture investment. Here, the SBIC may invest with long-term debt, while the venture arm may invest in common stock, a nice combination where needed.

SPECIALTY SBICs

There are some SBICs set up specifically to make investments in one industry. Some of these industries include: real estate development, broadcasting, fast-food franchises, movie production, grocery stores, just to name a few.

Unfortunately, most SBICs are small. The normal loan amount may be only $100,000 to $200,000 per portfolio company. Because of this the larger investment opportunities are often syndicated, which means several SBICs may invest together in the company. Usually, one SBIC plays a "lead investor" role and the borrower meets principally with them. A group of SBICs can put up $3 million without too much trouble. Over $5 million may be difficult to arrange.

It will pay a potential borrower to do his homework on specific SBICs to recognize specialties and areas of particular interest. Some like retail trade while others will invest only in manufacturing. So to better find the SBIC which will understand the needs of a small business, it's wise for the small businessman to know the SBIC he is approaching. With this background let's turn to the second principal form of financing through the SBA: SBA partially guaranteed loans.

SBA GUARANTEED LOANS

Probably 2,500 banks in the United States make SBA 90% guaranteed loans and there are a few non-bank companies which can handle such financings. Even with this large number, only several hundred lending institutions are actively making SBA guaranteed loans. Recently, the SBA selected 251 of the most active with the best loan records to be designated as "Certified Lenders."

As a Certified Lender, the SBA attempts to give three-day turnaround service. Further, the paperwork necessary for a loan has been reduced substantially, thereby reducing the processing time dramatically. (In Allied's case, it reduced the processing time from eight to twelve weeks to one to two weeks.) Thus, in these cases, an SBA guaranteed loan takes no longer than a regular loan. The small businessman wanting to utilize a guaranteed loan is advised to contact their local SBA office for a list of Certified Lenders. This listing may also be obtained from the Deputy Director of Finance, Small Business Administration, 1441 L Street NW, Washington, D.C. 20416.

The chief benefits from an SBA guaranteed loan are (a) better and longer terms and (b) enough money.

BETTER TERMS

Most lending institutions will not lend long-term, but on SBA guaranteed loans, much of the risk of a long-term loan is shifted to the SBA. SBA gives lenders an incentive to go longer-term by giving the lender permission to charge a higher interest rate on loans over seven years. The maximum terms are seven years for working capital, 10 years for machinery and equipment, and 20 years for real estate.

Interest rate maximums are on two scales: (1) a variable rate has a maximum of 2¾% over prime and changes quarterly; or (2) a fixed rate set at 2¾% over prime at the time the loan is submitted and stays at that rate. Thus, when the loan is submitted to the SBA lender, the fixed rate maximum that the lender can propose to the SBA is 2¾% over the current prime rate. Remember these are the maximums, the lender can always charge less.

ENOUGH MONEY

Because of the SBA guarantee, the lender can provide more money than conventional financial institutions. It is not uncommon for a small business to receive 100% financing on land and buildings where the small business lacks the standard down-payment funds. The same is true on machinery and equipment.

To some extent, working capital loans guaranteed by the SBA have been abused. The program is not set up for revolving lines of credit and is oriented to long-term loans. Some banks have tried to make term loans secured by accounts receivable and inventory, but have found it difficult to monitor and manage when the inventory and receivables rise and fall. The best use of SBA guaranteed loans is for long-term asset financing and the program is oriented to that end.

The maximum loan amount that can be made under the guaranteed loan program is $500,000. While this is usually sufficient for a small business it's not adequate for a growing business. There is a movement afoot in Congress to change the maximum to $750,000.

In summary, both SBA programs can benefit a small business. SBA loans can provide long-term debt financing for specific assets, while SBIC financing can provide growth capital.

Community Development Corporations and Economic Development Commissions

FREDERICK J. BESTE III

Over the past decade, community development corporations (CDCs) and economic development commissions (EDCs) have provided equity, debt, and grant financing to (or for the benefit of) large numbers of small- and medium-sized businesses. Although they are little known to most seekers of such capital, CDCs and EDCs are often more flexible and reasonable as to terms than are more conventional sources of financing. In addition, many prefer startup financings and are willing to back lower upside potential, non-proprietary situations.

The principal keys to attracting capital from such organizations are a convincing business plan and being in the right place (or being willing to go there), for both CDCs and EDCs are geographically restricted and seek to provide capital not only for traditional financial return (in the case of CDCs), but also for the economic development impact that will result from businesses being successfully spawned and expanded in these underdeveloped investment areas.

Businesses already located in such an area, or willing to establish a branch operation there, as well as entrepreneurs willing to start a firm there, would be wise to consider the often attractive financing available from CDCs and EDCs.

COMMUNITY DEVELOPMENT CORPORATIONS

In the broadest sense, CDCs are organizations charged with addressing the development needs of a geographically defined community. Needless to say, there are hundreds of ways to approach such a broadly defined task, and at least as many organizations that call themselves CDCs. In this article, however, we will discuss the 40 CDCs that receive grants from the Federal Government's Community Services Administration under legislation originally drafted in the mid-1960s. They range in location from Alaska to Massachusetts to Florida, and in geographic area from a few thousand acres to thousands of square miles.

This program is unique in that federally granted funds are used by CDCs to make venture capital type investments, *the ownership of which does not rest within the federal government, but within a private development corporation* governed by a board of directors composed of local business and community leaders.

CDCs operate under broad and widely varying charters as drafted by their individual boards of directors based on the characteristics and needs of their geographic areas, all of which are characterized by high unemployment and low income levels. In addition to their business development activities, the CDCs located in urban, inner-city areas often also become involved in housing development and/or rehabilitation projects; those located in rural areas are typically hampered by the lack of significant social and/or economic infrastructure such as shopping malls and industrial parks, and therefore sometimes assist in the financing of these types of projects.

As a result of the wide range of challenges in their different operating areas, each CDC has, within the intent of the legislation, set its own goals and priorities. A number of CDCs, Kentucky Highlands among them, focus on venture capital type investments. Others do not. A number of CDCs have elected to focus on large-scale property development; others have concentrated on purchasing control positions in their ventures, or on starting businesses themselves, which they then own in their entirety.

Increasingly, however, CDCs have selected a venture capital investment approach as their principal development technique.

QUALIFICATIONS FOR ATTRACTING CDC FINANCING

Geography is of course the most limiting factor with respect to attracting CDC investment capital. There is generally a lack of existing prosperous businesses located within the operating area of a CDC. For such firms, the establishment of a manufacturing branch plant or distribution center in such an area may, however, be possible. CDCs are spread all over the country and many are located where labor rates and relations are unusually attractive. (The locations of CDCs can be obtained from the Community Services Administration, Washington, D.C.)

Entrepreneurial startup situations are much easier for CDCs to address and are of prime interest to most of them. Even if you do not now live in an operating area of a CDC, there may be one close enough for you to be able to locate your plant nearby and commute (most CDC-backed firms are manufacturers). Alternatively, you may conclude that a move to a rural area would give you an opportunity to combine your separate dreams of living in the country, where you can keep a pony in the backyard for your kids, while attracting the kind of financing needed to build your business dream. Entrepreneurs desirous of attracting startup financing for a non-proprietary manufacturing firm may find that such a move represents their only financing alternative—traditional venture capitalists seldom back such companies.

There are other, lesser obstacles to attracting CDC financing. Some CDCs focus their investment activities on members of a predominant ethnic group, if there is one, in their operating area. Others, including Kentucky Highlands, are completely unrestricted in this respect. Some are located in areas where the lack of abundant skilled labor or support services would preclude certain types of businesses. Others, notably CDCs located in urban areas, have no such problems. Lastly, highly automated industries are generally less attractive to CDCs since job creation is usually a priority goal.

Without pretending to be inclusive, the profile of a typical CDC investee would be a business that is (1) interested in branch plant or distribution expansion, or is a startup, (2) headed by an experienced and committed entrepreneur or team, (3) involved in low to medium technology or relatively labor-intensive manufacturing and, (4) seeking $150,000 to $750,000 in initial risk capital.

It is significant that this profile gives financial indigestion to most sources of equity capital. Their argument is that it features high risk (startup businesses) and low return (labor-intensive businesses). The CDC industry's answers to these arguments focus on risk reduction and objectives.

First and foremost, the support of a town or community can go a long way toward reducing some of the risk of startup. Since a venture's success directly benefits a well-defined group of local citizens, the community as well as its leaders and institutions stand behind a CDC's venture in such areas as labor relations, business introductions, and local financing. The CDC itself, having generally worked with local individuals and institutions on similar projects for many years, can often assist in performing minor miracles in such areas as industrial revenue bond sales, vocational training programs, and in making many other inroads so often critical to a venture's prospects for success.

Additionally, some excellent talent can be found on the staffs of many CDCs. Backgrounds range from the venture capital industry to consulting firms to Wall Street investment bankers. Sound business counsel from such as these can be invaluable, yet is almost always provided without charge with CDC financings.

A last but important risk reducer for most CDCs is their strong capital bases. CDCs have the financial wherewithal to provide backup as well as second- and third-round support to their ventures, a strength that entrepreneurs often forget about (to their later chagrin) when raising funds from non-institutional sources. In the case of one successful firm, Kentucky Highlands followed an initial round of $220,000 of equity-oriented financing with four rounds of expansion financing totaling $1,080,000, all but $80,000 of which was straight debt.

As for limited upside, at least two points should be made. First,

CDCs are not in the game solely for the financial reward. While they would like to be able eventually to sell their investments at a profit to enable them to reinvest these funds in several new businesses, their performance is measured in various ways other than profitability. *Of course, CDCs realize that unless their investees are run with an absolute emphasis on profitability, any social benefits are illusory and short-lived.* Second, the emphasis on startup investments provides some of the upside capital gains potential missed by focusing on more mundane businesses. Kentucky Highlands' investment in the recreational tent manufacturer, Outdoor Venture Corporation (OVC), has become an almost classic example. OVC may be mundane, it may be labor intensive, and it may be addressing an established industry—but from rank startup eight years ago, it has grown steadily to a very substantial sales level and has been consistently profitable. There is significant unrealized appreciation in the OVC stock held by Kentucky Highlands and OVC's other founding shareholders, and all expect ultimately to cash in through a merger or public offering.

ADVANTAGES OF DEALING WITH A CDC

In some respects, dealing with a CDC offers some unique advantages, including the following:

1. Startups, traditionally almost impossible to finance, are the backbone of some CDC's business development strategy.
2. CDCs are essentially always in the market for new venture investments. Being long-term and startup oriented, they regard recessions as mandates and opportunities to get new businesses up and ready to take advantage of better times ahead.
3. The backing and considerable support of the surrounding community are automatically built into every CDC venture.
4. CDCs have virtually unlimited flexibility with respect to deal structure and the handling of unusual aspects of financings. In addition, given the duality of their goals, they are likely to provide somewhat more attractive terms than a traditional venture capitalist.

DISADVANTAGES OF DEALING WITH A CDC

A CDC financing generally has the following disadvantages:

1. Operating in underdeveloped areas can create problems, as there are usually good reasons why they are targeted for economic development initiatives. Urban CDCs are close to big city conveniences, but the business itself will not be in one of the better sections of town. Rural CDCs often feature beautiful countryside, but "Big 8" accounting firms and symphonies can be 50 to 100 miles away.
2. Local work forces have on occasion been known to require patience before stabilization and high productivity rates are possible. There are, however, notable examples to the contrary. As in other places, this principally depends upon personnel policy forethought and execution.
3. In general, CDCs move even more slowly than venture capitalists do, although a lot hinges on the timing of the receipt of a completed business plan. A minimum of two to three months is generally required from the date of introduction to investment.

DEALING WITH A CDC

Dealing with a CDC is not very different from dealing with a traditional venture capitalist. Observing the following pointers should enable you to maximize your chances of obtaining a CDC investment:

1. Determine beforehand by directory, reference, or phone calls which CDC or CDCs would be interested in a venture of your type. As previously noted, some CDCs do not make venture investments at all.
2. Come prepared. If possible, prepare your business plan in advance of your initial CDC meeting. If not, prepare a "miniplan" highlighting the opportunity, your background, and

the capital required. Incidentally, CDCs will expect you to be making a sizable personal investment relative to your net worth.
3. Be candid about your business and personal goals. They may conflict with the goals of the CDC, and it is important to spot any differences early. For instance, the CDC may be interested in selling out after a few years, while the entrepreneur may want to be involved in the business longer; a "put" from the CDC to the entrepreneur some years out or an Employee Stock Ownership Plan (ESOP) buyout could be the solution. Resolution of such differences is almost always possible if both parties are forthright and fair.
4. To the extent possible, try to address the needs of the community in your business plan. The timing of work shifts, promotion policies, types of fringe benefits offered, and care about many other areas over which management has considerable latitude can be successful in one locale and resented in another. Work with community leaders to find out what makes the most sense in your area.
5. Check with the managers of other ventures backed by the CDC to see how they feel about the area and their relations with the CDC now that some time has passed. Find out what kinds of difficulties have arisen and how they were resolved, whether any work force problems have developed, and, in general, what kind of a partner the CDC has been.

ECONOMIC DEVELOPMENT COMMISSIONS

Regional economic development commissions are a 1965 federal outgrowth of the existing Appalachian Regional Commission (ARC) concept whereby one central federally supported organization coordinated and provided various types of funding support for the relatively homogeneous Appalachian section of the country. Each of the 11 EDCs established since 1965 addresses the development needs of a large, multi-state geographic area that is culturally, historically, and economically similar across its breadth. At the present time EDCs cover, or will soon cover, the entire country with the exception of parts of Michigan, Minnesota, and Wisconsin.

Operated through funding provided by the U.S. Department of Commerce, these commissions seek to promote economic development in their designated regions by "reducing or removing obstacles to growth through planning, research, technical assistance and supplemental funding of Federal grant-in-aid programs." The principal program categories of EDCs include: (1) industrial development, (2) human resource development (particularly worker training), (3) energy conservation and development, (4) natural resource development, (5) transportation development, and (6) tourism and recreation development.

EDCs are precluded from providing funds directly to individual corporations and can only provide grants for situations that are *eligible* for grants from another federal agency such as the Farmers Home Administration or the Economic Development Administration. Business-related fundings tend to focus on infrastructure projects and are generally funded through an EDC grant to another governmental entity, such as a city or county. Typical EDC-funded projects would include industrial parks or water and sewer lines. For example, to the extent that a business proposing to locate in one of the EDC areas lacks a suitable plant site or the site lacks utilities, grant funding could be available to provide these from an EDC to the city, usually as a supplement to a grant from another, larger, federal agency. EDC participation is usually in the $50,000 to $150,000 range and rarely exceeds $500,000.

The notable business-related activity of EDCs that does not relate to infrastructure involves job training programs in which EDCs provide grants to local educational institutions (vocational or otherwise) to perform job training for a specific industrial purpose.

Locational and other information on EDCs is available from the Office of Regional Development of the U.S. Department of Commerce, Washington, D.C.

SUMMARY

CDC and EDC financial backing is not suitable for or available to everyone, but for those firms in the right place, and for those willing to initiate a new operation there, the financing can be extremely attractive, as can secondary benefits such as labor force characteristics, near-patriotic community support, and job training funding. The success stories are there to be replicated.

The MESBIC Connection: Venture Capital for the Forgotten Entrepreneur

WALTER M. MC MURTRY, JR.

That minority enterprise small business investment companies (MESBICs) have grown steadily in size, number, and wisdom is testimony to their strength.

MESBICs started when Robert Dehlendorf, then president and chief executive officer of the Arcata National Corporation of Palo Alto, California, proposed, and his board accepted, a plan to inject 2% of Arcata's net profits into an investment company. The year was 1968, the 2% of net profits amounted to about $150,000, and the investment company he proposed would operate on a simple investment philosophy.

"What we will try to do," Dehlendorf said, "is to back the right man with the right idea in the right marketplace." This time, however, the right man was to be a minority entrepreneur. Arcata National also planned to invest an additional $150,000 each year for the next five years. If this plan had been followed, Arcata Investment Company (AIC) would have had a private capital base of $900,000 by 1972. Today, the largest MESBIC has $4.7 million.

AIC, of course, had not yet become a MESBIC. It was happy to join the SBIC program, which the Small Business Administration had operated since 1958. In August 1968, Arcata Investment became a chartered SBIC, the only SBIC—out of more than 500—to specialize in venture capital for the minority business community.

Now it seemed that everybody was interested. The SBA had barely handed AIC its small business investment company license before the White House heard about it.

On November 6, 1969, President Richard M. Nixon announced "Project Enterprise," a key ingredient of which was something called a MESBIC. Very quickly—too quickly it now seems—everyone in the government became active. The President issued his Executive Order. The SBA was charged with licensing, regulating, and leveraging this new industry. A special Office of Minority Business Enterprise within the Department of Commerce was asked to stimulate interest in MESBICs as it went about implementing the President's general directive.

Even Secretary of Commerce Maurice Stans promoted MESBICs, and especially AIC, as he spoke to corporate and business audiences around the country about minority economic development. Stans envisioned the creation of 100 MESBICs by June 1970 and another 400 within the next several years. If this goal could be met, he argued, over a billion dollars would be available for minority business investment by the mid-1970s.

In mid-1980, however, 120 MESBICs have raised only approximately $84 million in private capital, a pool that the SBA has increased by another $92 million by purchasing debentures and non-voting preferred stocks.

MESBICs did not sprout like mushrooms under that plan. They did not even enjoy the boom regular SBICs experienced from 1958 to 1964. The reasons are obvious and represent a stage of growth the industry is glad to have behind it. Business and banking investors responded with too much financial caution and too little real commitment in terms of time and "hands on" assistance to MESBICs and their portfolio companies. Philanthropic groups were committed, but imprudent. No one won: you cannot invest just a little money on a "social" problem—nor are noble objectives a substitute for a good accounting system and hard cash.

AIC, which started as the first MESBIC, soon illustrated what could go wrong. It restricted its minority small business operations to "mom and pop" operations. Loans ranged in size from

$10,000 to $25,000, and either the loans were not adequately monitored or the management and marketing assistance did not arrive in time. In any event, too many of these businesses were lost, and AIC soon found itself depleted of operating capital. It stopped making loans in 1971.

Since 1979, the SBA has required a minimum of $500,000 in private capital commitment for all SBICs and MESBICs, but our own experience suggests $1 million to $2 million is needed to establish a viable venture capital company, and it takes considerably more to make them truly effective. SBICs have learned this the hard way. After 20 years, SBICs have finally turned profitable as an industry, but they lost approximately two-thirds of their original members doing it.

MESBICs are still part of the SBIC industry, but they have their own special investment charter and focus. MESBICs are privately owned venture capital companies licensed to provide debt and equity financing to small business firms that are at least 51% owned by socially or economically disadvantaged persons, such as members of minority groups.

- *Loans with warrants*—In return for a loan, the borrower issues warrants to the MESBIC to purchase common stock in the business at a specified price during a fixed period of time.
- *Convertible debentures*—The MESBIC receives a debenture in exchange for a loan. The debenture can be repaid with interest or converted to an equivalent amount of common stock in the business.
- *Common stock*—The MESBIC purchases common stock equity in the business.
- *Preferred stock*—The MESBIC purchases preferred stock in the business. This stock can be repaid through redemption or converted to common stock equity.
- *Straight loans*—Although the MESBIC usually will want the opportunity to share in the growth and potential profits of the small companies it finances, it will in some cases make loans involving no equity features. Interest rates, terms of repayment, and collateral requirements are determined by negotiations subject to state laws and SBA regulations. Loans can be for a minimum of 30 months, but five years is the usual minimum.

In almost all cases, a MESBIC provides management assistance to the clients it finances. This is an extremely important supplement to financing and may prove as valuable to the small business owner as the financing itself. Second- and third-round financings are possible with a number of MESBICs, especially when the investor has had ongoing involvement.

MESBIC deals range across the entire business landscape. Independence Capital Formation, the MESBIC of which I am president, has invested in such diverse industries as banks and fast food operations, a rubber manufacturer, a toy manufacturer, a railroad, and automobile dealerships. Other MESBICs have been involved in the communications, service, and transportation industries; in wholesale distribution, and in other ventures. When financing larger deals, such as the recent acquisition of a CBS-affiliated television station in Rochester, New York, several MESBICs joined in a syndicate, with one of them taking the lead. In these larger deals, MESBICs act as a catalyst for attracting traditional lenders. Their equity then becomes subordinated debt to a senior lender (in this case, the Chase Manhattan Bank). Last year, MESBICs made 441 financings for a total of $35.1 million. Almost 40% of those deals were startup situations, but the current economic climate argues that MESBICs, like other venture capital firms, move more toward expansion financing and acquisition of existing businesses.

Individual MESBICs set their own investment patterns. They also determine their maximum loan size and concentrate in certain business areas while taking no interest in others. Qualified entrepreneurs should put their packages together well, then check with several MESBICs before concluding that MESBICs "don't know a good deal when they see one." The industry has outgrown its old reputation as the "banker of last resort" for the minority community.

By law, MESBICs are prohibited from participating in most real estate transactions, cannot invest in nonprofit organizations or in individual projects (as opposed to ongoing businesses), and, of course, MESBICs cannot do business with a firm that is part of the MESBIC itself.

MESBICs can now be limited partnerships, but most are structured as private for-profit corporations subject to state usury law ceilings. MESBICs have not offered their own stock for public sale as the Narragansett Capital Corporation and other regular SBICs have chosen to do, but some MESBICs are discussing this option. The businesses MESBICs invest in can, of course, offer public stock, and that is a financing option that should be discussed with the MESBIC and any other investors.

What can minority businesses do to ensure a sympathetic hearing from MESBICs? Here are some suggestions:

- Have a strong knowledge of the industry in which you will be doing business
- Have a strong knowledge of the market area you will be servicing
- Have a sound management team
- Have a sound operational plan for success, which is the most important factor

The American Associations of MESBICs, located at 915 Fifteenth Street, NW, Washington, D.C. 20005, publishes a monthly newsletter and bi-monthly bulletin on the MESBIC industry that will keep the entrepreneur abreast of developments in the industry. Successful businesses are not created quickly, but MESBICs are committed to a more equitable opportunity for all enterprising Americans.

Corporate Venture Capital

KENNETH W. RIND

INTRODUCTION

Corporate venture capital generally differs from conventional venture investing in that motivations beyond strictly financial reward are present. Typically, a corporation will be seeking to gain exposure to new markets/technologies, generate new products, identify/assess acquistion candidates, assure a source of supply, and/or assist a customer. Corporations also may utilize venture capital concepts initiating new ventures internally, or in spinning off businesses which are not appropriately kept inside. Though corporate venturers represent only a small part of the venture capital community, their importance is growing and their involvement in the electronics industry in particular has been out of proportion to their size. This article will describe the unique benefits as well as the problems an entrepreneur will have in dealing with a corporate venture capital source.

HISTORY OF CORPORATE VENTURE CAPITAL

Probably the first corporate venturer was DuPont. When one of its important new customers ran out of funds in 1919, it purchased a 38% equity interest and brought in a new president, Alfred Sloan. General Motors has grown substantially since that investment. After World War I, American Telephone, General Electric, and Westinghouse bought out the British interests in American Marconi and subsequently changed the name of their company to Radio Corporation of America, now RCA.

Right after Second World War, a small company, Haloid Corporation, funded the commercialization of a new technology developed by Chester Carlson and the Battelle Memorial Institute. Haloid later changed its name to Xerox Corporation.

Another corporate venturer probably became interested in the concept because its largest stockholder was a man whose father had previously been the venture capitalist behind the formation of IBM. Fairchild Camera and Instrument financed a group of eight technologists leaving Shockley Transistor in 1957 and formed Fairchild Semiconductor, the grandfather of many of the companies now populating Silicon Valley.

Many corporations became active venture capitalists in the 1960s seeking a "window on technology." However, the lack of profit orientation and the decline of the market in 1970 brought about the exit of most of those established corporate venture capitalists, including such major names as DuPont, Ford, Alcoa, Union Carbide, Northrop, Scott Paper, and Singer, as well as some newer venturers such as Memorex, California Computer, Data Products, Boothe Computer, Electronic Memories, Mohawk Data, and Applied Magnetics.

Public interest in the stock market recovered in 1971 and 1972, before almost collapsing entirely in 1974 and 1975, driving many other corporate venturers from the business.

CORPORATIONS BECOME MORE ACTIVE

In the last few years there has been a renewal of interest in direct corporate venture capital investments, fueled by excess corporate liquidity, a relentless toughening of anti-trust oversight, and a desire to keep pace with technology developments. In addition, the entry of foreign corporations into the field has become a major new factor.

It is estimated that today there are more than 20 industrial corporations which directly invest over $200 million annually in ventures. This figure includes funds only under direct control. There has also been a growing tendency for corporations to invest in venture pools managed by others, both as a supplement to their direct investments, as well as a first step into the area.

A particular focus has been foreign corporations who have recently invested in semiconductor manufacturers in order to ensure available supply. The success of such attempts remains to be proven, but the trend has not yet abated.

Some noteworthy companies that presently have or have had participation by corporate venture capitalists include:

- *Computers*—Amdahl, Cray, Tandem, Wang, Apple, Qantel, Modular Computer
- *Medical Electronics*—Cordis, Coherent, Bentley Labs, Orion Research
- *Telecommunications*—M/A-COM, MCI, Telenet, Valtec, Paradyne, Quotron, Tran
- *Terminals*—Four-Phase, Datapoint, ADDS, Ramtek, Computer Communications, Centronics, Qume
- *Peripherals*—Documentation, Braegen, Data Royal
- *Instruments*—Waters Associates, Nicolet
- *Miscellaneous*—Radiation Dynamics, Data Card, Scope, Key Pharmaceutical, Xidex

PROBLEMS OF THE CORPORATE VENTURE

Although financial rewards are usually a secondary concern, corporate venture capital funds that have been run by professionals, even if not strictly for maximum return, have performed as well as any fund, with reported compounded annual returns of 20%-60%.

On the other hand, many corporations have failed as venturers. A recent survey of corporate venture capital organizations made by Tektronix states that only 7% of corporate venture capital organizations regard themselves as being very successful, with over half not even rating themselves as marginal successes. The difficulties experienced by a corporation seeking to become a venture capitalist usually arise from one of these sources.

Lack of Appropriately Skilled People

A venture capitalist must be entrepreneurially motivated, patient, realistically optimistic, good at negotiation, persuasive, and able to evaluate people as well as businesses. Also he must be more than merely familiar with accounting principles, tax regulations, corporate finance structures, securities analysis, and securities law. Good internal people are generally unwilling to leave a company's mainstream activities even if possessing the appropriate skills. Experienced people from the outside are difficult to attract and retain without special compensation packages which are almost impossible to structure.

Contradictory Rationales

A corporate venture capital program may find it difficult to act in the best interests of both the investee company and the parent. For example: if the goal of the venture group is to acquire, then equity financing by others is undesirable; if the rationale is an exclusive marketing arrangement or a preferred supplier role, then the investee's operations may be unduly limited. A desire to have continuous profit increases by the parent is also incompatible with the normal results of a venture operation.

The entire problem can be exacerbated by an improper reporting structure. For example, having the venture group report to the Vice President of Finance is likely to shift focus to profitability; to the Vice President of R&D to technology; to the Vice President of Corporate Planning to market information, etc.

Legal Problems

A corporate venturer must be extremely careful to organize its activities so that they will not run afoul of conflict of interest problems, including "fiduciary responsibility" and "corporate opportunity" doctrines. Several corporations have left the field incorrectly believing that legal constraints were inhibiting the strategic benefits they wanted out of a venture activity.

Inadequate Time Horizon

A venture activity usually shows its losses and problems early, with the successes taking more time to develop than anticipated. Unless a commitment is made for at least seven to ten years, a corporate venture fund generally gets terminated in its early stages.

SELECTING A CORPORATE PARTNER

In order to assure the viability of your long-term relationship, you should consider the following points:

Compatibility of Goals

As previously noted, corporations make venture capital investments for diverse reasons, including assisting potential suppliers or customers, gaining exposure to new technologies/markets, growing possible acquisitions, and obtaining a financial return. The business interests of both parties can either reinforce the possibility of success or lead to future conflicts.

Longevity

Many corporate venture groups have been shut down due to lack of early success, a failure to set clear objectives, or even just shifts in strategy. A failure of continuing support will probably arise at a poor time in the economy for raising funds from others. Make sure there is a true long-term commitment to the concept.

People

If the corporate group is not managed by experienced venture capitalists unnecessary conflicts may develop. Also, there may be a desire for the staff to return to a career path inside the corporation, thereby requiring continual efforts at education. Finally, the corporation may not provide adequate financial resources to build an independent operation.

Flexibility

The route necessary for decision-making may be short or tortuous. It is essential for the investee corporation that the venture group have appropriate autonomy to ensure that crises can be met quickly. Major corporations often measure performance against a set plan, whereas entrepreneurs must have the flexibility to react and restructure a plan to overcome a myriad of unexpected problems.

Interference

Unless the relationship is well-structured, the corporation may attempt to require its conventional reporting and staff policies which are inappropriate for a venture situation. Curiosity visits may also be a problem.

Time Horizon

Not all corporate venture capitalists realize the length of time that may be necessary to bring a new business to profitability. If your investors do not react rationally to unforeseen slippage, then the venture could experience substantial difficulty.

Style

Corporate venture groups, like noncorporate ones, differ in attitudes, approaches, and interests. A feeling of sympathy, which should have developed before the investment, is generally extremely helpful to a successful relationship and must be fostered in the aftermath.

CORPORATE INVESTORS BRING ADVANTAGES

Corporate venture capitalists believe they should be preferred investors. In addition to the usual financial and strategic assistance given by conventional venture capitalists, corporations also can offer:

- Assistance in almost all facets of corporate endeavor, e.g., setting up financial systems, qualifying suppliers, meeting government regulations;
- Credibility with customers, banks, and other investors both from a technical and financial standpoint;
- Relief, if desired, from the full range of corporate activities, e.g., the corporate investor may take on marketing responsibilities or may license the product;
- Immediate income from a R&D or consulting contract if appropriate;
- Customer interface with an interested party;
- An investor with an infinite lifetime, though his time horizon for profitability will be shorter;
- Additional capital where warranted;
- A merger partner, if and when appropriate;
- A more flexible financing package since return on investment may not be the only criterion.

CONCLUSION

Corporate venture capitalists can be good partners. However, it is fair to point out that there have been many abrupt terminations of such groups even when they have shown extremely good returns. Thus, the entrepreneurial team must investigate the venturing group just as carefully as they are investigated.

HOW TO RAISE VENTURE CAPITAL

This section is a step by step guide to obtaining venture capital financing. Written by experienced venture capitalists, each article explores one of the practical considerations in dealing with the venture capital process. Beginning with guidelines for contacting and working with venture capitalists, the articles continue with an outline of the type of detailed business plan that will facilitate a venture capitalist's investment decision, and the discussions offer entrepreneurs guidance in approaching the venture capital community and presenting the business plan, anticipating the pricing and structure of the financing, and understanding the legal requirements. The articles also point out what the venture capitalist is looking for, what he seeks to avoid, what will be required of the entrepreneur, and how the investment decision is made. Examining the venture capitalist's objectives and decision-making processes, together with the structured business plan, should help the entrepreneur to locate and build a productive investment relationship.

Guidelines for Dealing with Venture Capitalists

STANLEY E. PRATT

The relationship between entrepreneur and venture capital investor is unique, though often tenuous, and it can be a very significant factor in determining the success of a business development. Often referred to as a marriage, the venture capitalist/entrepreneur association, as any union, can achieve common purposes if the partners complement and support each other's capabilities, respect and understand different perspectives, and develop intuitive sensitivity to each other's actions and reactions. Successful rapport contributes to the "value added" that differentiates business development from passive investment and helps achieve the substantial rewards envisioned from venture capital investment.

Experienced venture capitalists should be viewed as a resource that goes beyond the provision of investment capital. The extent to which the benefits of professional venture capitalist involvement is realized depends upon the quality and chemistry of the relationship between a business' operating management team and the venture capitalist.

INITIAL CONTACT

It is important to begin the relationship with the venture capitalist on the right foot. For the entrepreneur there are several important "dos" and "donts" to keep in mind.

It is important to give serious consideration to which venture capitalist should be approached for funding a particular type of venture. If the entrepreneur devotes insufficient time and thought to selecting prospective venture capital investors, he wastes the time and money of both the entrepreneur and the venture capitalist. More importantly, venture capitalists can be turned off if they feel a deal has been too aggressively "shopped around" and consequently turned down by several of their peers.

Therefore, it is first advisable to find out which venture capital firms are looking at new proposals. How old is the particular venture funds? Is it fully invested? Is it looking for new situations to invest in, or is it reserving funds primarily for later-stage investments in existing portfolio companies? What size investment does the firm feel comfortable with? What are its stated interests in terms of industry and geographical preferences? In what types of businesses, stages of development, and geographic locations has it made prior investments? These kinds of questions are useful screening devices to locate the best possible matches between the entrepreneur and the venture capitalists.

The most desirable way to approach a venture capital firm is through an introduction from an individual or organization that is respected by the venture capitalist. This may be a banker, a lawyer, or an accountant who has brought them investment situations in the past, or other associates or intermediaries.

It should be emphasized, however, that in the venture capital industry there are few intermediaries who have been consistently effective. Venture capitalists are investing, more than anything else, in a management team, and the role of the intermediary operating between the venture capitalist and the management team is therefore delicate and can be counterproductive. It is easy for an intermediary to oversell the entrepreneur's capabilities and excessive involvement by the intermediary can lead to a suggestive perception of shortcomings in the management team. To be most effective, intermediaries should perform carefully measured services—introduction, advice, and guidance—but they must remain out of the limelight. Few professional intermediaries have the desire, interest, or ability to perform this delicate role since financings for, and acquisitions of, established businesses generally produce a greater compensation fee with less effort.

Without a personal introduction, it is probably best to send a letter with a brief (two or three page) summary of the business plan and to follow this up with a phone call. If the venture capitalist is interested in the potential investment, more information can then be provided.

Once a venture capitalist is seriously considering investing in your firm, overtures to other venture capitalists should be limited. While discussions should be maintained with several venture capital groups to discern market conditions and to find compatible future partners, emphasis must be placed upon working out an acceptable transaction, rather than on continuing a search for an investor who might accept preconceived conditions. Constructive feedback from all contacts should be considered to help fashion a mutually acceptable transaction. Remember that the proper financing of a business is generally the first, and often the most critical, selling effort made by a management team—today's customer may be tomorrow's partner.

PRESENTATION

The heart of the presentation is a written business plan through which the venture capitalist evaluates the potential development of a business and the capabilities of a proposed management team. Venture capitalists are constantly exposed to innovative and exciting new products, but products don't make a business—successful businesses create and develop successful products. The management team must demonstrate an understanding of the market and an ability to thoroughly think through and evaluate the actions in its business plan to attract the attention of venture capitalists.

The business plan, together with management's discussion of it, enables potential investors to focus upon management's planning skills and experience. It must be a product of the principal managers, rather than a polished exposition by outside consultants, since it documents management knowledge and expertise in the disciplines necessary for independent business development. It should combine a historical factual review with careful research and understanding to produce a realistic future plan. It is not a selling document, but shows the anticipated developments and the structures necessary to enable financing the proposal. Finally, it provides a mechanism for measuring potential and actual progress. Most business plans presented are far too optimistic, but those that are too conservative will not attract an investor's attention. It is thus important to present reasonable expectations that both the management and the venture capitalist can accept as achievable.

Perhaps the most important part of the business plan and its presentation is the clear identification of the existing and future market needs as well as the niche that will allow a business to exist and successfully expand. Too often, entrepreneurs are enthusiastic about a marvelous product and they expect the potential investor to recognize the product's need without documentation as to why or how the customer will purchase the product. The professional venture capitalist knows that it is the nuts and bolts details that enable a product to achieve commercial success.

Present the business plan, and yourself, in a natural manner because this is the best way to demonstrate your knowledge. The presentation must not be a high powered dog and pony show evidencing your remarkable sales abilities.

This is not a customer you can walk away from once you have received the order and have delivered your product. If successful, you will be living with this customer, your future partner, for an extended period through both good and bad times. You will be seen at your best and your worst so present yourself as you really are. Be confident in what you can deliver but not arrogant. Experienced venture capitalists have been there before and they are comfortable with the process of financing businesses. Raising new capital is a traumatic experience to most operating managements but if presentations are made with adequate homework, facts are presented to avoid unpleasant surprises, and a natural and realistic exposition is made, the proper chemistry may be developed with venture capitalists to bring about a remarkable amount of assistance even prior to any final decision.

INVESTIGATION

Perhaps the most frustrating aspect of dealing with venture capitalists is the time required during the period from original introduction to the closing of an investment. Realistic planning should allow for at least three to six months for contact, courtship, and investigation. When a business needs funds yesterday, the process is even more problematic and only the most intuitive venture capitalists will respond. Adequate investigation and familiarization takes time, and venture capitalists are just as busy and jealous of time as operating managements. Time frames should be discussed initially and reasonable schedules should be set up and maintained. One of the best ways to judge a venture capitalist's interest is in the time allocated for substantive investigation.

After an initial meeting, the responsible venture capital firm will indicate within a week or two whether it is interested in seriously considering a proposal. If so, the investigation begins in earnest with extensive checking of the management, an analysis of product, technical and marketing considerations, and a financial analysis. While these studies require a great deal of time and effort on the part of both parties, they are necessary to establish the understanding required for long-term involvement; and an entrepreneur generally benefits from such a review.

At the same time, the entrepreneur should be conducting an investigation and analysis of the venture capital firm. Some investors can offer a great deal more than others, especially in specific industries or in particular stages of business development. The experience and expertise of the investor should be carefully reviewed. Perhaps the best way to check on venture capitalists is to contact the managements of other companies in which the venture capitalist has invested. This should include successful businesses, as well as disappointing experiences and outright failures, to determine how a potential investor will react to both good and bad developments. The nature and frequency of communications between the venture capitalist and the managements of portfolio companies should be noted. In general, the entrepreneur should seek strong rather than passive investors, much the same as venture investors desire to back strong management teams. It is critical to determine each side's capacities to establish mutual trust and working relationships.

NEGOTIATIONS

Once the investigations have been completed the final details of the investment are subject to the give and take of direct negotiation. Usually the negotiations are handled by the chief executive officer of the operating management team and the venture capitalist. Advisors such as attorneys and accountants can be helpful, but decisions cannot be delegated since management must live with final determinations during the difficult times of building a business. Generally, compromise is necessary for both parties and it is important that both sides feel that a fair deal has been reached. Each side must leave a little bit at the table and not burden the relationship with unrealistic projections or expectations. If unrealistic expectations are created initially, the entrepreneur will be suffering from a credibility gap right from the start. An open and honest relationship will reduce the number of surprises later.

Too often, entrepreneurs confuse ownership with control. Management controls a business and the venture capitalist's role is generally supportive—enabling greater growth than might have been accomplished without such involvement. If a business fails to develop in accordance with planned expectations, venture capitalists as owners may push for changes through the board of directors. Directors may seek changes in the controlling management of the business, but ownership positions in developing businesses are seldom responsible for such restructuring. Most often, venture capitalists operate through persuasion in the expectation that their original decision on a management team was correct.

The structure of a financing determined in these negotiations must be clearly understood by all parties. The amount of capital investment is usually determined with the expectation that additional funds will be made available in a series of steps that are dependent on the development of the business. The use of debt and equity will be structured in accordance with the requirements and capabilities of the business as well as the objectives and needs of the investor.

Depending upon the stage of development of the business being financed, the venture capitalist seeks a potential return of five to ten times his investment and a means of ensuring future liquidity. Factors relating to these liquidity requirements are a part of the venture capitalist's negotiating objectives.

The most important point to remember about the negotiations is that, while there may be disagreements, the overall tenor of the negotiations will often set the tone for ongoing relationships.

THE CONTINUING RELATIONSHIP

The entrepreneur should strive to delineate his own objectives and understand those of the venture capitalist. This facilitates discussions around those objectives, particularly in the early stages. Objectives change with time and different conditions, and it is necessary to air and discuss these changes to determine how the relationship might be affected. The most important point is to "stay close" and to "keep on top of each other's thinking." Continuing communication is critical to maintain an ongoing productive relationship.

The entrepreneur should learn as much as possible about the venture capitalist's capabilities and should attempt to exploit these talents to create opportunities and solve problems. This is the essence of how the venture capitalist adds value to investments.

The common trait differentiating professional venture capitalists from other investors is long-term, ongoing involvement—they are not normally passive investors. Enhanced returns are expected through the value added by specialized, experienced assistance. Independent business development requires unique skills that may not have been necessary in the larger corporation where the entrepreneur acquired management training. Venture capitalists provide assistance in: policy determination for small, growing businesses; long-range planning; financial assessments and arrangements; management evaluation and recruitment; relations with outside technical consultants and vendor/suppliers; relations with shareholders; and provisions for the eventual liquidity of ownership positions. With this valuable assistance available to, and focused on, the entrepreneur, it is incumbent upon operating managements to maintain working relationships to take advantage of that experience and expertise. There may be times when one side or the other is difficult to convince, but a frank, ongoing relationship produces the value added to investments that creates extremely rewarding business partnerships.

Preparing a Business Plan

BRIAN HASLETT and LEONARD E. SMOLLEN

Before you begin in earnest to develop the comprehensive business plan that you will need to raise venture capital, you should try to convince yourself that:

- You are indeed an entrepreneur with *some* demonstrated management ability.
- You have a viable idea for the startup or expansion of a business that is selling in a market that you (or a partner) have preferably worked in or at least have studied thoroughly.
- You can secure the commitment of one or two other people, whose skills and experience complement your own, to work with you to build your business.

Developing a business plan that will attract the professional venture investors' interest and, more important, their financial commitment is a major challenge because you are likely making such a plan for the first time. Even those with a good business education may well not have learned how to put together a comprehensive business plan. To *ease* the entrepreneur's task, Brian

Haslett and Leonard Smollen, two of the founders of Venture Founders Corporation, Waltham, Massachusetts, prepared the detailed guidelines that follow. They interviewed many successful venture capitalists about their experiences and used their own experience in analyzing numerous venture proposals in writing this article. Their aim is to help the entrepreneur comprehend the scope of what is required and appreciate how much detail is needed to establish the fundamentals on which a good startup or expansion are based.

VFC's staff has been working with entrepreneurs in the various parts of the U.S. since 1972,[1] helping to develop their management teams and business plans. Though entrepreneurs often find this process of building teams and preparing plans harder and more lengthy than they anticipate, those who "complete the course" are generally able to raise the capital they need and proceed to moving their businesses ahead successfully. Their financing comes from different sources—private capital funds, corporate venture capital, and community development corporations, a source of early-stage investment capital of which few are aware.

Businesses that have been developed with this assistance range from manufacturers of tents and kayaks in Kentucky and of rock drilling equipment in Florida, to a manufacturer of thermal glass for windows and a remanufacturer of mining tools. All of these businesses were planned with guidelines similar to those set out below. Two of them are already profitable multi-million dollar corporations.

USING THESE GUIDELINES

When raising equity capital, your business plan is a vital sales tool. Before risking their money for what may be a period of five years or longer, most venture capital investors will want to satisfy themselves that you have thought through your plan carefully and

[1] Originally published and copyrighted (1972) by the Institute for New Enterprise Development (INED). Revised for this book by the authors, founders, and principals of Venture Founders Corporation (VFC), Waltham, Massachusetts.

that you and your associates have enough skill and experience in your chosen business area to manage effectively, seize opportunities, solve problems, *and* make profits. These prospective backers will—or should—insist on reviewing your proposal *before* considering any investment seriously. Some will not even meet with an entrepreneur without first seeing his business plan. For this reason, your plan must be well-prepared and very persuasive in conveying the potential of your company. It should cover all major issues and yet not be so detailed that the investor–reader is "turned off." Fifty pages should suffice for most businesses.

Use common sense in applying to your particular business the guidelines described here because they are meant to cover a wide variety of manufacturing and service businesses. It is not possible or desirable to follow them slavishly. For example, a plan for a service business will not require a discussion of manufacturing or product design.

When starting up or expanding a business in your particular industry or market, there are certain currently critical issues of which you ought to be aware and with which you must deal in your plan. In the chemical industry, issues of significance can, for example, include the following:

- Reduced availability of raw materials and resultant bartering and allocation
- Increasingly strict regulations at all government levels, covering the use of chemical products and the operation of chemical processes
- Diminishing viability of the high capital cost, special-purpose chemical processing plant serving narrow markets

Make whatever investigations are needed to develop a list of special issues that are related to your business.

These guidelines, because they contain a list of potentially *relevant* issues, may help you develop your list. But it is up to you to determine which issues are, at the time you are preparing your plan, *significant* to the future development of your business.

Professional venture capitalists are not the only people who find business plans invaluable. For the entrepreneur, the careful preparation of a plan is an important opportunity to think carefully through all of the facets of a business expansion or startup, to examine the consequences of different marketing, operations, and financing strategies, and to determine what human, physical, and financial resources are required. Much of this *can* be done effectively on paper without the expense of trial-and-error operation.

In one venture that we helped develop, the discipline of writing his business plan caused the entrepreneur to realize that the major market for his biomedical product was in nursing homes, not in hospital emergency rooms as he had previously supposed. He changed the focus of his marketing effort accordingly.

Another successful entrepreneur with whom we worked has told us that, besides his plan to help raise $650,000 startup capital, it helped him monitor his company's performance during its first 18 months. Then, when he needed to increase his company's credit lines, and to secure long-term financing for building and equipment, he was easily able to update his plan.

SUMMARY OF THE PLAN

Many investors like to read a one- or two-page summary of a business plan that highlights its important features and opportunities so that they can quickly decide if it is worth their while reviewing the whole plan carefully. Do not write your summary until you have written your plan. As you draft each section of the plan, circle a few sentences that you think are important enough to be included in a summary.

Allow plenty of time to write an appealing and convincing summary. Remember that this summary is probably the first thing about you and your business that the would-be investor is going to read. Unless it is appealing and convincing, it may also be the last!

We suggest that your summary should contain *very brief* statements about

1. your company's activities, management, and performance,
2. any distinguishing features of your product or service,
3. the attractiveness of your market,
4. a summary of your financial projections,

5. the amount of money you now seek, in what form (equity or debt or both), and for what purpose.

We suggest that you persuade several people to review your summary while it is still in draft form. They should be people whose business realism you respect, but who are not involved in your venture. Then evaluate their reactions realistically. Did they quickly grasp what you are proposing to do? Were they "turned on" by what they read? Did they ask you how much stock you are willing to sell them? They should provide you with some useful indications of how the professional venture capital investor is likely to react.

DESCRIPTION OF YOUR BUSINESS AND ITS INDUSTRY

In this section, you should provide the reader with some background for what you are going to present in subsequent sections about your product/service, your market opportunity, and the people and plans that you have for going after that opportunity. You should *briefly* describe what product or service you are offering, to whom, and the nature and current condition of your industry to show where you fit in it.

Your Company

Describe the business you are in or intend to enter. Describe your product/services, possible customers, and regions of operation.

Trace the history of your business: when it was formed; how its products/services were chosen and developed; and what roles each of the principals played in bringing the business to where it is today.

If your company is already trading and is now seeking further development or expansion financing, review its operations history and financial performance (sales, profits, return on equity). If, as is quite normal, your company has had early setbacks and losses, describe these and say what you are doing to avoid recurrences. Omission of any reference to past problems can make your proposal appear too good to be true.

Your Industry

Present your view of the current status and prospects for the industry in which your businesses do, or will, operate. Describe the principal participants and how they are performing, growth in sales and profits and also any published forecasts for the current year, companies that have recently entered or left these markets and why, and what major economic, social, technological, or regulatory trends are affecting your business. In this section you should not go into too much detail. That is done later.

FEATURES AND ADVANTAGES OF PRODUCTS OR SERVICES

The potential investor wants to know *exactly* what you are going to sell, what kind of protection you have, and what the opportunities and drawbacks are.

Description

Describe, in more detail than previously, the products or services that you sell or intend to sell and what needs they satisfy. Use diagrams, sketches, and pictures if illustration will improve understanding and interest. Emphasize any distinctive features of your product or service by highlighting the differences between what competitors currently have on the market and what you have or will offer. State candidly each feature's advantage or disadvantage.

Proprietary Position

Describe any patents, trade secrets, or other proprietary features. Discuss any head start that you have or could have that would enable you to achieve a favored or entrenched position in your industry.

Potential

Discuss any opportunities for the logical extension of your existing line or the development of related products or services. Investors like to know what you can do for an encore.

MARKET RESEARCH AND ANALYSIS

In this section of your plan, you should present enough facts to convince the investor that the market for your product or service is such that you can achieve your sales target in the face of the competition. The discussion and the guidelines below should help you do this.

This is probably the most difficult section for entrepreneurs to do well. And, because choice of marketing strategies, size or operating work force and facilities, and requirements for inventory and receivable financing all have to be closely related to sales forecasts, it is also the most crucial. Because of this, we advise you to prepare this section of your business plan *before you do any other* and to take enough time to do it really well.

Customers

Define your markets clearly. Explain who the major purchasers for your product or service are, where they are, and why they buy. Discuss and indicate by rank order the significance or price, quality, service, personal contacts, and political pressures. When do they buy? Discuss the significance of seasonality—when the buying is done, and how it affects your offering.

List some actual or potential customers who have purchased, or expressed an interest in, your product or service and indicate why. List any actual or potential customers who have dropped, or shown no interest in, your product or service, and explain why this was so. Explain what you are doing to overcome negative customer reaction. The absence of some frank discussion about the negatives of your offering leads readers to wonder if you are telling your whole story.

Market Size and Trends

What is the size of the current total market for the product you have or service you do or will offer? This market should be determined from discussions with potential distributors, dealers, sales representatives, and customers, as well as a review of whatever published data are available. Don't rely solely on published data.

It is often inadequate and known to be so by industry insiders. Give the size of the total market in both units and dollars. Be careful to include *only* the market you are in fact going after. If you intend to sell regionally, show the regional market size.

Describe the potential annual growth of the total market for your product or service. Market projections should be made for at least three future years. Discuss in more detail than previously how the major factors, such as industry trends, new technical developments, new or changing customer needs, are affecting market growth and review previous trends of the market. Any differences between past and projected future growth rates should be explained. If you are assuming that past trends will continue, say why. Entrepreneurs tend to overestimate the size of their market. If potential investors become dubious about your market size and growth estimates, they may lose interest in the rest of your proposal.

Competition

Make a realistic assessment of the strength and weaknesses of competitive products and services and name the companies that supply them. State the data sources used to determine which products are competitive and the strengths of the competition.

You should compare your products or services with your competitors on the basis of price, performance, service, warranties, and other pertinent features. A table can be an effective way of presenting these data.

Then review the managerial and financial strengths and weaknesses of your competitors. Give your assessment of each competitor's capability in marketing, operations, and finance, and their recent trends in sales, market share, and profitability. If they are not doing well, explain why you expect to succeed.

Conclude this section by explaining why customers buy from your three or four key competitors. Then, from what you have presented above about their operations, explain why you think that you can capture a share of their business—*if* that is how you plan to grow.

Entrepreneurs often know less about their competition than they should. Professional investors are very wary of proposals in which competition is treated lightly.

ESTIMATED MARKET SHARE AND SALES

Identify any major customers who have made or are willing to make purchase commitments. Indicate the extent of these commitments.

| | | Sales and market share data ||||||||
| | | 1st year |||| 2nd year ||||
		Q1	Q2	Q3	Q4	Q1	Q2	Q3	Q4
Estimated total market	Units								
	Dollars								
Your estimated sales	Units								
	Dollars								
Your estimated market share	Units								
	Dollars								

Estimate the share of the market and the sales in units and dollars that you think that you can achieve. Base this estimate on your assessment of your customers and their acceptance of your product or service, your market size and trends, and the competition, their offerings, and their share of sales in prior years. The growth of your sales and your estimated market share should be related to the growth of your industry and customers and the strengths and weaknesses of your competitors. The data should be presented in tabular form, as shown above. If yours is an existing business, also indicate the total market, your market share, and sales for two prior years.

Marketing Plan

Your marketing plan should describe *how* you will achieve your sales target. The marketing plan should include a description of your sales and service policies and pricing and distribution and advertising strategies that will use to achieve your goal. The marketing plan should make clear *what is to be done, how it will be done,* and *who will do it.*

Marketing Strategy

A description of your marketing strategy should include a discussion of the kinds of customers who will be targeted for initial heavy selling effort, customers who will be sought for later selling efforts, method of identifying specific potential customers and of contacting them, and the features of the product or service (quality, price, delivery, warranty) that will be emphasized to generate sales.

If the sales of your product or service are seasonal, discuss this and indicate any ideas you have for obtaining out-of-season sales.

Pricing

Many entrepreneurs, after convincing the investors that they have a superior product, then say they intend to sell it for less than their competitors. This makes a bad impression for two reasons. First, if their product is as good as they say it is, the entrepreneurs can be judged as poor sales people if they have to offer their product at a lower price than the competition. Second, costs do tend to be underestimated. If you start out with low prices, there is little room to maneuver if costs run over budget. Price hikes are tougher to make stick than price cuts.

Your pricing policy is one of the more important decisions you make. Your "price must be right" to penetrate your market, maintain your market position, and produce the profits you project. Devote enough time to considering a number of pricing strategies and convincingly present the one you select.

Discuss the prices to be charged for your product and service and compare your pricing policy with those of your major competitors. Explain how the price you set will enable you to:

- secure/increase acceptance of your offering,
- maintain and desirably increase your market share in the face of competition, and
- produce profits.

Justify any price increases over competitive items on the basis of newness, quality, warranty, and service. If your product is to be priced lower than your competitors' products, explain how you will do this and maintain profitability.

Sales Tactics

Describe how you will sell and distribute your product or service. Do you or will you use your own sales force, sales representatives, and distributors? Are there ready-made manufacturers' sales organizations already selling related products that you already use or can use? If distributors or sales representatives are used, describe how they have been or will be selected, and the areas they will cover. Discuss the margins to be given to retailers, wholesalers, and your commissions to sales representatives, and compare them to those given your competition. Describe any special policies regarding such items as discounts and exclusive distribution rights.

If a direct sales force is being introduced, indicate how it will be organized and at what rate it will be built up. Show the sales expected per salesman per year and what commission incentive and/or salary they will receive. Explain how these figures compare to those of your competition.

Service and Warranty Policies

If your company will offer a product that will require service and warranties, indicate the importance of these to the customer's purchasing decision and discuss your method of handling service problems.

Advertising, Public Relations, and Promotion

Describe the program you will use to bring your product to the attention of prospective customers. Indicate your plans for public relations, trade show participation, trade magazine advertisements, direct mailings, and the preparation of product sheets and promotional literature. If advertising will be a significant part of company expenses, details of how and when these costs will be incurred should be presented.

DESIGN AND DEVELOPMENT PLANS

If any of your products or services require design and development before they are ready to be placed on the market, the nature and extent of this work should be fully discussed. The costs and time required to achieve a marketable product or service should be indicated.

Such design and development might be the engineering work necessary to convert a laboratory prototype to a finished product, the design of special tooling, the work of an industrial designer to make a product more attractive and salable, or the identification and organization of manpower, equipment, and special techniques to implement a service business, for example, the equipment, new computer software, and skills required for computerized credit checking.

Development Status and Tasks

Describe the current status of the product or service and explain what remains to be done to make it marketable. Describe briefly the competence or expertise that your company has or will acquire to complete this development. Indicate the type and extent of technical assistance that will be required, and state who will supervise this activity within your organization, and give his experience in related development work.

Difficulties and Risks

Identify any major anticipated design and development problems and approaches to their solution. Discuss their possible impact on the timing of the market introduction of your product or service and the cost of design and development.

Costs

Present and discuss a design and development budget. The costs should include labor, materials, consulting fees, etc. Design and development costs are often underestimated. This can seriously impact cash flow projections. Accordingly, consider and perhaps show a 10%–20% cost contingency. These cost data will become an integral part of the financial plan.

OPERATIONS PLAN

The operations plan should describe the kind of facilities, space requirements, capital equipment, and labor force (part and full time) that are required to provide the company's product or service. For a manufacturing business, discuss your policies regarding purchasing, "make or buy decisions" (which parts of the product will be purchased and which operations will be performed by your work force), inventory control, and production control. A service business should describe the appropriateness of location, and lease of required equipment, and competitive productivity from a skilled or trained labor force.

The discussion guidelines given below are general enough to cover both product and service businesses. Only those that are relevant to your venture—be it product or service—should be used in preparing the business plan.

Geographic Location

Describe the location of the business and discuss any advantages or disadvantages of the site in terms of wage rates, labor unions, labor availability, closeness to customers or suppliers, access to transportation, state and local taxes, state and local laws, utilities, and zoning. For a service business, proximity to customers is generally a "must."

Facilities and Improvements

If yours is an existing business, describe the facilities currently used to conduct the company's business. This should include plant and office space, storage and land areas, machinery, special tooling, and other capital equipment.

If your venture is a startup, describe how and when the necessary facilities to *start* production will be acquired. Discuss whether equipment and space will be leased or acquired (new or used), and indicate the costs and timing of such actions. Indicate how much of the proposed financings will be devoted to plant and equipment. These cost data will become part of the plan.

Discuss how and when plant space and equipment will be expanded to the capacities required for future sales projections. Discuss any plans to improve or add to existing plant space or to move the facility. Explain future equipment needs and indicate the timing and cost of any acquisitions. A three-year planning period should be used for these projections.

Strategy and Plans

Describe the manufacturing processes involved in your product's production and any decisions with respect to subcontracting component parts rather than manufacturing them in-house. The "make or buy" strategy adopted should consider inventory financing, available labor skills, and other nontechnical questions as well as purely production, cost, and capability issues. Justify your proposed "make or buy" policy. Discuss any surveys you have completed of potential subcontractors and suppliers and who these are.

Present a production plan that shows cost–volume information at various levels of operation with breakdowns of applicable material, labor, purchased components, and factory overhead. Discuss the inventory required at various sales levels. These data will be incorporated into cash flow projections. Explain how any seasonal production loads will be handled without severe dislocation, for example, by building to inventory, using part-time help, or subcontracting the work.

Briefly, describe your approach to quality control, production control, and inventory control. Explain what quality control and inspection procedures the company will use to minimize service problems and associated customer dissatisfaction.

Discuss how you will organize and operate your purchasing function to insure that adequate materials are on hand for production, that the best price and payment terms have been obtained, and that raw materials and in-process inventory and hence working capital have been minimized.

Labor Force

Explain, exclusive of management functions (discussed later), to what extent the local labor force has the necessary skills in sufficient quantity and quality (lack of absenteeism, productivity) to manufacture the product or supply the services of your company. If the skills of the labor force are inadequate for the needs of your company, describe the kinds of training that you will use to upgrade their skills. Discuss how your business can provide and pay for such training and still offer a competitive product both in the short term (first year) and long term (two to five years).

MANAGEMENT TEAM

The management team is the key to a successful business. Investors look for a committed management team with a balance in marketing operations and financial skills and experience in doing what is proposed.

Accordingly, this section of the business plan will be of primary interest to potential investors and will significantly influence their investment decisions. It should include a description of the key management personnel and their primary duties, the organizational structure, and the board of directors.

Organization

In a table, present the key management roles in the company and name the person for each position.

Discuss any current or past situations in which the key management people have worked together that indicate how their skills complement each other and result in an effective management team. If any key individuals will not be on hand at the start of the venture, indicate when they will join the company or what you are doing to locate and secure commitments from such individuals.

In a new business, it may not be possible to fill each executive role with a full-time person without excessively burdening the overhead of the venture. One solution is to use part-time specialists or consultants to perform some functions. If this is your plan, discuss it and indicate who will be used and when they will be replaced by a full-time staff member.

If the company is established and of sufficient size, an organization chart can be appended as an exhibit.

Key Management Personnel

Describe the exact duties and responsibilities of each of the key members of the management team. Include a brief (three or four sentence) statement of the career highlights of each individual to focus on accomplishments that demonstrate ability to perform the assigned role.

Complete résumés for each key management member should be included here or as an exhibit to the business plan. These résumés should stress education, training, experience, and the accomplishments of each person in performing functions similar to that person's role in the venture. Accomplishments should be discussed in such concrete terms as profit and sales improvement, labor productivity gains, reduced operating costs, improved product performance, and ability to meet budgets and schedules. When possible, it should be noted who can attest to accomplishments and recognition or rewards received, such as pay increases and promotions.

Management Compensation and Ownership

The likelihood of obtaining financing for a startup is small when the founding management team is not prepared to accept initial modest salaries. If the founders demand substantial salaries in excess of what they received at their prior employment, the potential investor will conclude that their psychological commitment to the venture is a good deal less than it should be.

State the salary that is to be paid to each key person and compare it with the salary received at his last independent job. Set forth the stock ownership planned for the key personnel, the amount of their equity investment (if any), and any performance-dependent stock option or bonus plans that are contemplated. Mention any loans made to the company by management, indicating on what terms they were made and under what circumstances they can be converted to equity.

Board of Directors

Identify board members and include a one or two sentence statement of the member's background to show how he or she can benefit the company and what investment (if any) has been made.

Management Assistance and Training Needs

Describe candidly the strength and weaknesses of your management team and board of directors. Discuss the kind, extent, and timing of any management training that will be required to overcome any weaknesses.

Supporting Professional Services

State the legal (including patent-counsel), accounting, public relations, advertising, banking, and other service organizations that you have selected for your venture. Supporting service organizations that are reputable and capable (remember reputations live on even after capability diminishes) cannot only provide significant direct, professional assistance, but can also add to the credibility of your business. In addition, properly selected professional orgainzations can help you establish good contacts in the business community, identify potential investors, and help you secure financing.

OVERALL SCHEDULE

A schedule that shows the timing and interrelationship of the major events necessary to launch the venture and realize its objectives is an essential part of a business plan. In addition to being a planning aid and showing deadlines critical to a venture's success, a well-prepared schedule can be an extremely effective sales tool in raising money from potential investors. A well-prepared and realistic schedule demonstrates the ability of the management team to plan for venture growth in a way that recognizes obstacles and minimizes risk.

Prepare, as a part of this section, a month-by-month schedule that shows the timing of activities such as product development, market planning, sales programs, and operations. Sufficient detail should be included to show the timing of the primary tasks required to accomplish each major goal.

Show on the schedule the deadlines or milestones critical to the venture's success. This should include events as follows:

- Incorporation of the venture (for a new business)
- Completion of prototypes. This is a key date. Its achievement is a tangible measure of the company's ability to perform.
- When sales representatives are obtained
- Dates of displays at trade shows
- When distributors and dealers are signed up
- Order of materials in sufficient quantities for full-time operation
- Start of operation. This is another key date because it is related to the production of income.
- Receipt of first orders
- First sales and deliveries. This is a date of maximum interest because it relates directly to the company's credibility and need for capital.
- Payment of first accounts receivable (cash in)

The schedule should also show the following and their relation to the development of the business.

- Number of management personnel
- Number of operations personnel
- Additions to plant or equipment

Discuss in a general way the activities most likely to cause a schedule slippage and what steps you would take to correct such slippages. Discuss the impact of schedule slippages on the venture's operation, especially on its potential viability and capital needs. Keep in mind that the time to do things tends to be underestimated —even more than financing requirements. So be realistic about your schedule.

CRITICAL RISKS AND PROBLEMS

The development of a business has risks and problems, and the business plan invariably contains some implicit assumptions about them. The discovery of any unstated negative factors by potential investors can undermine the credibility of the venture and endanger its financing.

On the other hand, identifying and discussing the risks in your venture demonstrates your skill as a manager and increases your credibility with a venture capital investor. Taking the initiative to identify and discuss risks helps you demonstrate to the investor that you have thought about them and can handle them. Risks then tend not to loom as large black clouds in the investor's thinking about your venture.

Accordingly, identify and discuss the major problems and risks that you think you will have to deal with to develop the venture. This should include a description of the risks relating to your industry, your company and its personnel, your product's market appeal, and the timing and financing of your startup. Among the risks that might require discussion are the following:

- Price cutting by competitors
- Any potentially unfavorable industrywide trends
- Design or operating costs in excess of estimates
- Sales projections not achieved
- Development schedule not met
- Difficulties or long lead times encountered in the procurement of parts or raw materials
- Difficulties encountered in obtaining needed bank credit line because of tight money
- Larger than expected innovation and development costs to stay competitive
- Lack of availability of trained labor

This list is not meant to be complete but only indicative of the kinds of risks and assumptions involved.

Indicate which business plan assumptions or potential problems are most critical to the success of the venture. Describe your plans for minimizing the impact of unfavorable developments in each risk area on the success of your venture.

THE FINANCIAL PLAN

The financial plan is basic to any investor's evaluation of your business and should represent your best estimates of future operations. Its purpose is to indicate the business potential of your venture and its capital needs. The financial plan should also serve as an operating plan for financial management of your business.

In developing your financial plan, three basic exhibits must be prepared:

- Profit and loss forecasts for three years
- Cash flow projections for three years
- Pro forma balance sheets at startup, semi-annually in the first year, and at the end of each of the first three years of operation.

In the case of an existing business seeking expansion capital, balance sheets and income statements for the current and two prior years should be presented in addition to these financial projections.

After you have completed the preparation of the financial exhibits, briefly highlight in writing the important conclusions that can be drawn. This might include such items as the maximum cash requirement, the amount to be supplied by equity and debt, the level of profits as a percentage of sales, and how fast any debts are repaid.

Profit and Loss Forecast

The preparation of your business' projected income statements is the planning-for-profit part of your financial plan. Crucial to the earnings forecasts, as well as other projections, is the sales forecast. The methods for developing sales forecasts have already been described in these guidelines, and the sales forecasts made there should be used here.

The following list is a group of headings that can be used in drawing up your profit and loss (P&L) forecast for prospective investors. Italics indicate items that should be included in the figures for that heading but not listed separately in the statement.

Sales
Less: Discounts
Less: Materials used
 Direct labor
Less: Bad debt provision
 Manufacturing overhead
  includes rent, utilities, fringe benefits, telephone
 Other manufacturing expense
  leased equipment, etc.
 Depreciation
Total cost of goods sold
 Gross profit (or loss)
Less: Sales expense
 Engineering expense
 General and administrative expense
  *office supplies, accounting and legal
  services, management, etc.*

Operating profit (or loss)
Less: Other expense
 (*e.g., interest*)
Profit (or loss) before taxes
Income tax provision
Profit (or loss) after taxes

Figures should be projected for three years. The first year should show a breakdown by months for each item. The second and third years should project quarterly figures. Figures for all three years should appear on a single sheet of ruled paper—make sure the paper you use is large enough. Tape two pages together, if necessary.

Once the sales forecasts are in hand, production costs, or operations costs for a service business, should be budgeted. The level of production or operation that is required to meet the sales forecasts and also to fulfill inventory requirements must be determined. The material, labor, service, and manufacturing overhead requirements must be developed and translated into cost data.

Sales expenses should include the costs of selling and distribution, storage, discounts, and advertising and promotion. General and administrative expenses should include management salaries, secretarial costs, and legal and accounting expenses. Manufacturing or operations overhead includes such items as rent, utilities, fringe benefits, and telephone.

If these earning projections are to be useful, they must represent your realistic and best estimate of probable operating results.

Discussion of Assumptions

Because of the importance of profit and loss projections, you should explain any assumptions that you made in their preparation. Such assumptions could include the amount allowed for bad debts and discounts and sales expenses or general and administrative costs as a fixed percentage of costs or sales.

Cash Flow Forecast

For a new business, the cash flow forecast can be more important than the forecasts of profits because it details the amount and timing of expected cash inflows and outflows. Usually the level of profits, particularly during the startup years of a venture, will not be sufficient to finance operating cash needs. Moreover, cash inflows do not match the outflows on a short-term basis. The cash flow forecast will indicate these conditions.

The following headings can be used in preparing the pro forma cash flow analysis. Like the income statement, the cash flow analysis should cover three years, with the first year broken down into 12 monthly figures and the second and third year projected by quarters. Again, this analysis should be made on a single large sheet of ruled paper.

    Cash balance: Opening
    Add: Cash receipts
      Collection of accounts receivable
      Miscellaneous receipts
      Bank loan proceeds
      Sale of stock
        Total receipts

Less: Disbursements
  Trade payables
  Direct labor
  Manufacturing overhead
  Leased equipment
  Sales expense
  Warranty expense
  General and administrative expense
  Fixed asset additions
  Income tax
  Loan interest @ ———%
  Loan repayments
  Other payments
    Total disbursements

Cash increase (or decrease)
Cash balance: Closing

Given a level of projected sales and capital expenditures over a specific period, the cash flow forecast will highlight the need for and timing of additional financing and show you your peak requirements of working capital. You must decide how this additional financing is to be obtained, on what terms, and how it is to be repaid. Part of the needed financing will be supplied by the professional venture capitalists, part by bank loans for one to five years, and the balance by short-term lines of credit from banks. This information becomes part of the final cash flow forecasts.

If the venture is in a seasonal or cyclical industry, in an industry in which suppliers require a new firm to pay cash, or if an inventory buildup occurs before the product can be sold and produce revenues, the cash flow forecast is crucial to the continuing operation of your business. A detailed cash flow forecast that you understand can enable you to direct your attention to operating problems without the distractions caused by periodic cash crises that you should have anticipated.

Discussion of Assumptions

This should include assumptions made on the timing of collection of receivables, trade discounts given, terms of payments to your suppliers, planned salary and wage increases, anticipated increases in any operating expenses, seasonality characteristics of the business as they affect inventory requirements, and capital equipment purchases. Thinking about such assumptions when planning the operation of your business is useful for identifying issues that may later require attention if they are not to become significant problems.

Balance Sheet Forecasts

The balance sheets are used to show the assets required in the operation of your business and, through liabilities, how these assets are to be financed. Investors and bankers look to the projected balance sheets for such information as debt to equity ratios, working capital, current ratios, and inventory turnover. The investor will relate them to the acceptable limits required to justify future financings that are projected for the venture.

The following headings may be used to prepare the balance sheet forecasts.

ASSETS

    Current assets
      Cash
      Marketable securities
      Accounts receivable
      Inventories
        Raw materials and supplies
        Work in process
        Finished goods
          Total inventory
      Prepaid items
        Total current assets

    Plant and equipment
      Less: Accumulated depreciation
    Net plant and equipment

Deferred charges
Other assets (identify)
  Total assets

LIABILITIES AND STOCKHOLDERS' EQUITY

Current liabilities
  Notes payable to banks
  Accounts payable
  Accruals
  Federal and state taxes accrued
  Other
    Total current liabilities

Long-term notes
Other liabilities

Common stock
Capital surplus
Retained earnings
  Total liabilities and stockholders' equity

Forecasted balance sheets should be prepared at startup, semi-annually for the first year, and at the end of each of the first three years of operation.

Cost and Cash Flow Control

Your ability to meet your income and cash flow projections will depend critically on your ability to secure timely reports on, and effectively control, your operating costs. For this reason, investors will want to know what kind of cost and cash control systems you have or will use in your business. The financial plan should include a brief description of how you will design, install, and maintain systems for controlling costs and cash flows appropriate to the nature and size of your business, who will be responsible for getting cost data, how often cost data will be obtained, and how you will take actions to reduce costs that are running higher than you expected.

PROPOSED COMPANY OFFERING

The purpose of this section of the plan is to indicate the amount of money that is being sought and to briefly describe the uses that will be made of the funds raised. The discussion and guidelines given below should help you do this.

Desired Financing

Summarize from your cash flow projections how much money you will need over the next three years to carry out the development and expansion of your business that have been described. Indicate how much of this money you expect to obtain now from the sale of stock and how much you think you can borrow from a bank. Describe the kind (common stock, convertible debenture, etc.), unit price, and total amount of securities to be sold in this offering. Also show the percentage of the company that the investors of this offering will hold after the offering is completed or after any exercise of stock conversion or purchase rights.

Capitalization

Show in a table the names of your current shareholders and the number of shares each holds. Also indicate how many shares of your company's common stock will remain authorized but unissued after the offering.

Use of Funds

Investors like to know how their money is going to be spent. Provide a brief description of how the capital raised will be used. Summarize as specifically as possible what amount will be used for such things as product development, capital equipment, marketing, and general working capital needs.

The Presentation and Other Key Elements

CHARLES P. WAITE

Although there may be a misconception in the business community that a strong and effective presentation is perhaps the most important factor in obtaining venture capital, I believe this idea is erroneous. A sow's ear can't be made into a silk purse; the project itself must be fundamentally good—a real opportunity to create a major entity—before any venture capital firms will be interested, regardless of the quality of the presentation.

It is essential that the entrepreneur carefully think through what he really wants to do. What kind of a company does he want to create? How large is it to be? What is initially required before the company can be created or a presentation developed?

It often appears that most businesses get started at cocktail parties where old college friends or people who once worked together in large companies meet. They compare notes and decide both are unhappy and want to start a business. But the entrepreneur must ask himself, "Is there a real need for the business?" Most venture firms want to back companies that have been started to fill a basic need. Once the need has been identified, the entrepreneur must then organize, structure, and develop the company in the most effective manner. Companies started over cocktails rarely have these fundamental qualities.

At Greylock & Co., we like to back people who have the reputation of being the best in their particular industry. A man's prior record in business is a critical element in the evaluation process. For example, it was clear when ARD backed Digital Equipment that its president, Kenneth Olson, was one of the two or three best people in the country to undertake the project.

It is also critical that the entrepreneur realize that he must make enormous sacrifices to create a major company. He will have to devote an inordinate amount of time to the business seven days a week and neglect his family, his hobbies, and most of his other interests. Although Greylock and most other venture capitalists look for a management team to back, there is usually one key man who is the spark plug of the team and who makes it function effectively.

After careful self-analysis, development of a basic concept to meet a need, and the formation of an active management team, specific attention must be devoted to the marketing strategy. What will cause the marketplace to sit up and take notice of the company? Is the product a really superior one that will attract business? Very few products are of this caliber. It is critical that the company have an effective marketing strategy if it is to establish itself quickly in the marketplace. At present, venture capitalists primarily back projects related to the industrial or commercial area. Businesses that rely on government contracting are relatively uninteresting. Marketing has therefore become a far more important element in the overall consideration of which types of projects to back.

THE PRESENTATION

The final element in the basic consideration is the presentation. The presentation should be made by the entrepreneur and the management team themselves and not by an intermediary, since it reflects the basic philosophy, capability, and intensity of the management team. While we have no bias against professionals reviewing the presentation or helping polish up a few of the rough spots, we feel that the basic work should be done by the management team itself.

Investment bankers can make the initial contacts and do the preliminary screening for venture capital firms, helping to introduce the entrepreneur and management team in an effective way. Once this has been done, however, it is up to the management team to carry the work forward and to convince the venture capitalist that the project and the quality of management are worth the support of the venture capital firm. Judicious use of investment bankers probably improves the chances of successful financing. It is difficult, however, to convince leading investment banking firms to sponsor such projects, since these firms must be almost as selective as the venture capitalists themselves. It is important to select investment banking firms that have specific experience with similar early-stage projects. Firms that specialize in underwritings for major corporations or in selling bonds would be inappropriate for this type of function.

In the presentation, the story of the project should be told in a straightforward, clear-cut way. The technological aspects of the business should be simplified so that, even though the venture capitalist does not have a degree in physics, he will understand the nature of the technology, the stage of its development, and its practical application.

ANALYZE THE MARKETPLACE

A key to the presentation is a thorough analysis of the market. Perhaps this is where most proposals are weakest. The entrepreneur must understand the dynamics of the marketplace in which he is trying to sell. He must know both the strengths and weaknesses of competing products and, specifically, why his product can replace others that are currently being bought. It is important to indicate both the size of the market and its built-in growth. Analysis of competitors must be sufficiently clear so that the venture capitalist can be convinced that the new company will be able to function effectively and out-compete existing products.

DESCRIBE MANAGEMENT

Key members of the management team must be described completely. The specific experience that makes them uniquely qualified for the job they are to do on the specific project must be spelled out in detail. What have they done in the past five years that particularly applies to the project? What kind of work were they actually doing for their previous employers that gave them this kind of experience? This description must be accurate because the venture capitalist will carefully check it. If there are any variances between the description in the proposal and actual experience, the venture capitalist is apt to drop the project.

A major aspect of the presentation is a discussion of the financial aspect of the project. If an existing business is involved, the financial data should include figures of the last three to five years. It is important that thorough discussion be made of the actual history of the business, indicating both its strengths and its weaknesses. If the company has lost money, the reasons for the loss should be analyzed as well as the reasons why injection of additional capital will turn such a loss into a profit.

Forecasts are an essential part of the financial presentation, and the forecasts should be done as realistically as possible. While very few venture capitalists fully believe projections, a management that does project accurately will build an effective business faster than anyone else. Such a business will receive major support in the financial community more quickly than others, and shares will usually achieve a much higher price earnings multiple; thus, additional financing will be easier and cheaper to obtain. Projections must be effectively supported by facts and by the external cash-generating capabilities of the business.

In addition to these general guidelines, I have developed the following do's and don'ts based on experience over many years.

1. Do disclose any significant problem with the company or the project at the initial discussion. Once the venture capitalist discovers the problem, he will instantly lose confidence if it has not been previously discussed. The venture capitalist must have implicit trust in the entrepreneur or management of the business.
2. Don't spend too much money on the brochure itself. If the brochure is too elaborate or slick, the venture capitalists become concerned that management is not financially conservative, or perhaps too promotion-oriented, and will run the

business in the same way. One key aspect in building up an early-stage business is to hold expenses to the minimum to conserve capital for unexpected problems and for expansion.
3. Don't bring your lawyer, accountant, or other advisers to initial meetings with the venture capitalist. Lawyers tend to talk too much, and often talk about the wrong things from the standpoint of the venture capitalist. While intermediaries can do an effective job of bringing parties together, they tend to create problems during initial discussions. It is far better for the venture capitalist to become intimately acquainted with key management people without any interference from others.
4. Don't press for a rapid investment decision. Venture capitalists do not like to hear that a project is being purchased very rapidly and that they have only a few days to make a decision. While the venture capitalist must respond within a reasonable period, the kinds of risks that are entailed in this business do not lend themselves to hasty decisions. Decisions are generally made within a period of three weeks to three months; the longer period applies mainly to projects with major problems, or to startups. Both require a great deal more time to investigate.
5. Don't sell the project on the basis that other venture capitalists have committed themselves to invest. Most venture firms take great pride in making their own decisions and will not be railroaded, regardless of which other venture firms are involved in the project. On the other hand, this information will be significant in the case of an otherwise attractive investment. The venture industry is small, however, and many of the people have some relationship with one another. There is a great deal of cross-checking between groups in the industry, and nothing would be more discouraging than a false representation that another venture firm had made a commitment when it had only indicated an interest.
6. Be flexible in pricing a project. Pricing is a complex subject, which varies significantly in different periods in the marketplace and, to a lesser extent, in different areas in the country. For example, there is some evidence that Boston investors and venture capitalists tend to look at projects somewhat differently from the way people on the West Coast do.

Bostonians tend to apply a fairly conservative price earnings multiple to investments in existing businesses. For an early-stage project, it is likely that when venture capitalists put up most of the money, they will receive considerably more than half of the equity. *In some ways, the stronger the venture capital firm, the tougher will be its position with regard to equity.* On the other hand, in many cases the strongest venture capital firm will be able to make a more significant impact on the growth of the business, thereby justifying its better equity position.

7. Be sure it is possible to review the actual background of the entrepreneur. Although this can be a very delicate exercise in certain situations, it is essential to evaluate a man's past performance in order to project his present and future capabilities. If for some reason it is not possible to discuss a man's capabilities with his prior employer, his customers, and a variety of other people who can provide information and insight, most venture capitalists will not be able to proceed further with the project.

Venture Financing Techniques

EDWARD F. GLASSMEYER

As part of his preparation for raising venture capital the entrepreneur should become familiar with the terms that are commonly contained in stock or debt purchase agreements.

The purchase agreement provides a mechanism for the investor to manage his liquidity risk. A private investment is not easy to sell, and investors will request a legally binding contract to give them the right to sell their stock when they have the opportunity, or to give them a senior position if the company is sold or liquidated on a distressed basis. Other provisions customarily sought by investors range from the right to demand a public offering to control of the board of directors if agreed-upon financial and operating tests are not met.

If the entrepreneur understands the investor's objectives, he can give some liquidity preferences to the investor in exchange for retaining a greater amount of ownership for himself. On the other hand, if he is sensitive about giving the investor too much control, he can offer more ownership to increase the investor's expected return, and at the same time lessen the need for a toughly worded purchase agreement.

TYPES OF INSTRUMENTS

Let us briefly review the major instruments for financing venture investments and highlight their relative strengths in providing liquidity for the investor. (In his discussion, assume the investor purchases less than 50% ownership in each case.)

Common stock is the most frequently used instrument for purchasing ownership in a company. It carries the right to vote on certain corporate decisions, and it can pay dividends, although it rarely does in venture investments. In liquidation, however, common stockholders are the last to share in the assets of the corporation. If the company is successful, shares can be sold through a registered public offering or sold without registration to the public under Rule 144, which is discussed later. Investors will insist that registration rights accompany common stock sold in private transactions.

Convertible preferred stock (convertible into common) provides the investor with rights that the common shareholder does not have. Terms are negotiated for each financing and can include access to internal financial data, as well as establish financial tests that, if not met, provide for control of the board of directors to shift to the investors. Investor liquidity is improved by virtue of the ability to influence the company through control provisions or by the attraction of an instrument with strong covenants to other investors.

Subordinated debt (either convertible or with warrants) is used in venture financing situations in which the investor wants the security and yield of a debt instrument, and the company does not want to restrict its ability to borrow from banks or insurance companies. If subordinated debt does not dominate the capital structure, it will be viewed as equity by senior lenders.

Subordinated debt gives the venture capitalist more options than does a straight equity position. If the company defaults on the loan, the investor can accelerate repayment, and if the company cannot repay, the venture capitalist (now a creditor) has strong leverage to influence management decisions.

Under Rule 144, an investor must hold an investment for two years before selling under the provisions of the rule. After this holding period investors in public companies may sell the greater of 1% of the total outstanding shares in any six-month period or the average trading volume for the four weeks preceding the sale.

Because the holding period does not begin until warrants are exercised, convertible debt is generally more attractive from a liquidity standpoint than debt with warrants.

Of the three instruments, the one that appears most attractive for both the purchaser and the issuer is preferred stock. On the one hand, preferred stock is equity and provides a sound base of the company's future growth. Customers, creditors, and suppliers are all interested in seeing a strong capital structure. On the other hand, if properly structured, preferred stock can contain rights virtually equivalent to those in a debt contract, which can assure the venture capitalist of a liquidation preference or the ability to influence key management decisions.

Preferred stock customarily pays dividends; however, some investors may defer dividend payments since they are paid with after-tax dollars, in contrast to interest, which is tax deductible. Most companies also have return opportunities that justify retaining cash in the business.

SELECTING THE APPROPRIATE INSTRUMENT

Selection of the appropriate instrument for each venture project will depend on a number of factors, two of the most important of which are the existing capital structure and the amount of ownership that can be purchased.

1. *The existing capital structure.* If the company has already sold three series of convertible preferred, for example, an investor is not likely to buy a fourth. He will probably demand that all of the preferred stock be converted into common stock in order to invest with a preferred stock instrument, or he may accept the capitalization as is, but invest with subordinated debt to retain a position senior to that of the prior investors. The most recent investor usually will seek precedence over the earlier investors.
2. *The amount of ownership that can be purchased with each instrument.* Generally an investor will purchase a greater ownership interest in a venture project if he uses the most junior instrument. If an investor is willing to give up the yield

and security of a debt instrument, he will want to purchase more of the equity of a company.

There are many trade-offs to be considered in choosing the appropriate instrument, but the venture capitalist is likely to choose the instrument that can purchase the most ownership of the company while offering strong liquidity provisions. These provisions may fall inside or outside the purchase agreement.

REGISTRATION RIGHTS

Registration rights provide the investor with a way to get liquidity if the company is successful and can attract a public market for its stock. Registration rights, in essence, are the rights of one investor or of a group working in concert to force the company to file a registration statement with the SEC, as the initial step toward achieving a public offering of the investor's shares. Greater liquidity can be achieved if the investor has the sole right to trigger registration without the approval of other investors or of the company.

Important issues to be negotiated regarding registration rights are (1) the dollar size of the offering, (2) the number of shares an investor can sell, (3) the payment for registration (including legal and accounting fees), (4) the right to participate in other company registrations (piggyback rights), and (5) the precedence of certain investors' shares if the size of the offering is reduced.

LIQUIDITY AGREEMENTS

If the company is unable to achieve a public market for its shares, what can the investor do as an alternative? Some possibilities are suggested here.

SIDE AGREEMENTS WITH MANAGEMENT

Side agreements at the closing of an investment can formalize understandings that can substantially enhance an investor's ability to realize the anticipated return on his investment. Many investors evaluate the prospects for the sale of the entire company when they make their initial investment. The sale of a minority position in a private company is extremely difficult, and therefore the venture capitalist will often reach an understanding with management regarding the conditions under which 50% or more of the business can be sold.

The following example presents a situation many investors have experienced: A third party has offered to purchase the investor's shares at an attractive price; however, the offer is conditioned on purchasing at least 50% of the company, since control and the ability to consolidate sales and earnings are critical to the purchase decision. To deal with this kind of issue, the venture capitalist might have negotiated a side agreement with the company whereby, given a minimum price and holding period, management would agree to use its influence to deliver 50% or more of the shares (including its own) or retire the investor's position at the proposed purchase price under a formula repurchase agreement. Repurchase agreements are particularly appropriate for financing family-owned businesses when there is a chance that management control will pass to members of the entrepreneur's family who have no interest in a public market for the company's shares.

PROVISIONS WITHIN THE PURCHASE AGREEMENT

Investors often negotiate certain rights as part of the purchase agreement to preserve the capital structure and limit changes that could affect both their ownership and their seniority in a merger or liquidation. For example, retaining the rights to approve a merger, or a sale of additional stock, works to control dilution and improve the investor's liquidity. The right to control the board of directors if certain performance tests are not met is probably the most powerful right a venture investor can negotiate to ensure a return on his investment.

Negotiating strong demand registration rights can provide the investor with a liquidity preference even if the company does not want to go public. The investor can waive his demand right on the condition that the company provide him with liquidity. Under such circumstances, the company must find a buyer for the investor's shares or repurchase them directly.

SINKING FUNDS

Sinking funds can be applied to both preferred stock and debt and will force the company to deal with the investors' liquidity needs if the investors have not converted their instruments into common stock and sold shares in a public offering. A sinking fund is a commitment to set aside funds to be used to retire a financial obligation. If the company meets its sinking fund payments, the investor will be "taken out" of his investment. If the company fails to make a sinking fund payment, it will be in default. Investors can then gain greater control and with it the potential to achieve greater liquidity.

DEFAULT

The investor will only exercise his rights under a purchase contract after some event has triggered a default or after the company has failed to meet a performance test. In most cases such an event cannot be followed by an immediate sale, but the investor can then set in motion a program to improve the liquidity of his investment. Such a plan may entail internal measures such as cutting back operating levels to preserve cash, or external actions, such as recapitalizing the company to improve the instrument held by the investor, soliciting a buyer, or implementing a program to raise additional funds.

CONCLUSION

The fundamental understanding and agreement on objectives between management and investor provide an excellent start for a venture investment. If their goals are in concert, management will work as hard as the investor to achieve their joint objectives—

establishing a public market, positioning the company for sale, or finding alternative means for all of the owners to realize a return. Each situation will have its unique characteristics, but a common understanding of the rights to be negotiated in the purchase agreement and of the trade-offs between financing with debt or equity should lead to the parties reaching an agreement that satisfies the objectives of both management and investor.

Structuring and Pricing the Financing

STANLEY C. GOLDER

STRUCTURING

It is the experience of the author that the structure of the financing can have a material effect on the eventual result of an investment and, therefore, the structure is an important element in setting the price. At times there are differences of opinion within the venture capital industry as to whether to purchase preference issues (such as convertible preferred stock, subordinated debentures, and notes with warrants) or to buy common stock. It is clear that new companies cannot afford to pay interest or dividends, and if the venture capitalist structures an instrument that calls for their payment, he is merely taking back his own money. In addition, consideration should be given to the fact that the balance sheet will be more appealing to other creditors and suppliers if the investment is in the form of common stock rather than debt instruments.

Although these are truisms, they do not address themselves to several key questions, one of which is the possibility that a company might move sideways, rather than up or down. If a company does not go public or sell out to a large company, but remains on a modest plateau, it is difficult for the private investor to recover an investment held in straight common stock. Even if the company goes public, the market will not accept a large amount of stock unless the company makes major progress. The only way out for the venture capitalist would be the sale of the company. The company managers do not have the problem to the same extent for, after all, they can receive high salaries and fringe benefits. They may be strongly opposed to the sale of the company.

To avoid this kind of stalemate, it has been the preference of many not to make an outright purchase of stock in a case in which management has the controlling interest in the business or can block the sale or merger of the business with a larger company. Before taking a common equity position, there should be some waiting period to see if the company performs as expected and to see if management has objectives similar to those of the venture capitalist and, therefore, will protect his interests as a minority shareholder.

The question of ultimate liquidity for the investment is also very significant. To deal with both liquidity and capital protection, the best financial structure entails a limited amount of money invested in common stock, with the rest employed in debentures, notes, or preferred stock. These instruments will provide some income and protection in case the business starts to decline. By having less dollars invested in common stock, the pressure to liquidate is reduced, allowing the venture capitalist time to find less painful ways to dispose of his holdings.

The third major problem is that of control. Most businessmen want to control their own businesses. The difficulty is that small-company management often consists of technical or sales people and there usually is not a well-rounded management team with depth of experience. The loan agreement or preferred stock indenture should give the management sufficient flexibility to run the business as long as things go reasonably well. On the other hand, such an instrument should give the investor an opportunity to exert pressures in case problems develop. Many people misunderstand the purpose of the terms of a loan agreement or preferred stock indenture. They presume that simply because a default exists, which could justify exercising the right to take control, the venture capitalist will immediately exercise such right. In fact, the record shows that this is rare.

There are major differences between investors. Not all money is the same in the venture industry, and nearly every group has different operating philosophies. While there may be a few waiting for a default in loan agreements so that they can take over a company, decrease their equity costs, or increase their percentage of ownership, the majority of venture capitalists do not have this attitude. This does not mean, however, that any of us are "patsies" or that we will not use appropriate remedies when necessary to protect an investment.

It is important for entrepreneurs to understand the general philosophies under which most venture capitalists operate. Loan agreement covenants are not the key aspect of pricing, but they do bear on the issue. Reasonable loan and preferred stock covenants are nothing more than a reflection of a good business plan. They often act as a disciplinary measure for management. This discipline is particularly important for young, growing companies, in which management often has a tendency toward exuberance.

Venture Capitalist vs. Entrepreneur

Naturally, there are some basic differences between the entrepreneur and the venture capitalist. The businessman is by nature an optimist and is enthusiastic about his ability to succeed. While the venture capitalist is not a pessimist (if he were, he would not be in this business), he can appropriately be described as a skeptic.

The businessman feels his company is worth more than does the potential investor. His projections show excellent growth over the next two to four years, and he believes that the investor should be willing to pay a high price to buy into this "bonanza." The venture capitalist, on the other hand, is skeptical because the young business simply has not proved whether its concepts and ideas will work. The business may be profitable, barely profitable, or, more likely, in a loss position at the time of investment. Competition can suddenly become much more disagreeable, or any number of other problems can arise to prevent a company from achieving its targets.

These major differences can raise major obstacles between

entrepreneur and venture capitalist when they discuss structure and pricing, and the differences often prevent their getting together. Yet the problem can be resolved, and techniques for structuring the investment have been developed to help bridge the gap. The following examples have been developed to illustrate the use of structuring for three types of situations.

As will become apparent, these methods are somewhat complicated, which fact can have a negative impact both on the future prospects of the company and on the relationship between the entrepreneur and the investor. *It is better not to have such a formula* but rather to keep the arrangements as simple as possible. However, in certain circumstances the techniques described below can be very helpful and the examples serve to outline approaches.

Resolving the Differences

Example 1 is a new company, so both entrepreneur and venture capitalist had a free rein in structuring the financing from the inception of the deal. After the entrepreneur's projections were modified by our analysis, it was decided that the company would need $1 million. The projections indicated that profits would be generated within the first year, an unusual expectation for a startup investment. Management, although capable and experienced, had nominal funds that could be invested; thus the venture capitalists initially would have voting control.

As the investors did have control, we were willing to invest in common stock. However, even if the projections were realized and a public market developed rather quickly, it would be impossible for the investors to sell all of their shares except over a long period of time.

This arrangement, by which the management can receive a maximum equity position through reaching its projections, is called an earn-out. Critical aspects of this transaction were the considerations under which the earn-out numbers were determined. Originally, the proposal was that the earn-out be based on an earnings formula for the first three years of operation, but this approach created problems for us as the venturers. Although there was no disagreement with the principle and although the formula was considered fair in practice, even if the company could meet its projections for three years, we would not have a value to show on the books or a gain that could be realized. In addition, it was important to focus the company management's attention on providing the investors with ultimate liquidity.

For these reasons, it was decided to use a market value formula to avoid an argument about the value of the company. The higher the earnings multiple placed on the shares by the market, the easier it would be for management to get its maximum percentage under the formula. While none of us wanted to create a premature public offering, it was generally agreed that sometime in the three-year period, market conditions would be such that the company could go public. A three-year period was chosen to give management flexibility in deciding when to go public.

If a public market had not been created at the end of that period (because of inadequate earnings growth or some other management-related problem), we considered that a multiple of five times net after tax earnings was appropriate for pricing the shares purchased. You will note that the valuation formula included a 30% discount from the public market price of the shares. This represented an estimate of the average discount appropriate for the nonregistered stock. Since the investors would own about 50% of the company, the shares could not be easily sold in the public market without a long holding period or considerable registration expense. The discount was considered appropriate to take these problems into account. (Actually, if such shares were sold in a private transaction, the discount could range from 25% to 50% of the price in the public market.)

Management's projections seemed reasonable to us, and in turn the managers agreed to a formula for pricing the equity that would be tied to the future profit performance of the business. In many cases this suggestion results in a severe downward revision of projections of profits by the entrepreneur.

A preferred stock issue backed by a sinking fund was created to provide liquidity for the investment. Because of the early expectation of profits, it was felt that this company could afford the sinking fund payments in years four through six without jeopardizing its equity position. If things worked out badly, we could have 82% of the equity. On the other hand, if projections were met, and the company were to go public within three years at a multiple of 10 times earnings or better, the investors would be cut down to 51% and management would receive 49% of the equity with only a nominal investment. We wanted management to have every possible incentive to bring the company to an optimum growth rate. However, the longer it takes the company to go public, the lower will be management's equity. We reasoned, too, that this move would protect our interests until the "earn-out" arrangement becomes effective.

The above situation was made somewhat easier because we were dealing with a brand new company without a previous capital structure. But imaginative structuring and pricing is also possible with existing businesses.

Beginning Capital Structure

6% Sinking fund preferred (sinking fund reduction in years 4-6)	$ 900,000
Class A common	102,500
Class B common	22,500
Total capital	$1,025,000

Class A shares initially represent 82% of the company ownership and can be diluted down to 51.25% if the earn-out formula is achieved. Class A shares are owned by the investor group.

Class B shares initially represent 18% of the company ownership, which votes on a share-for-share basis with Class A ownership and is subordinate to Class A in liquidation. Class B shares are convertible into Class A shares at the resolution of the earn-out and are owned by management.

Earn-Out Arrangement

The earn-out is based on the first public market price of the company, provided a public market is established in the third to fifth years. (A public market is defined as either (1) an offering in which at least 20% of the company is sold to the public or (2) a merger in which control is sold to a listed company.) Management will receive no more than 18% of the company until the value of the original Class A position meets the following values.

Time of first public offering	Class A value
Year 3	$5,000,000
Year 4	6,000,000
Year 5	7,000,000

If a public market is not established by the end of the fifth year, then for earn-out purposes an "internal" value will be calculated which is five times the lower of (1) average earnings in the third to fifth years or (2) fifth-year earnings.

Because of the restricted nature of the original Class A position, a 30% discount will be applied to the public market value for calculating the company value used for the earn-out formula. Assuming a public market is established in the third year, placing a value on the company of $12 million (or $8.4 million), and the management group would increase its position from 18% to 40.5% through conversion of Class B into Class A stock.

The company's projected after-tax earnings for the third through fifth years are as follows:

Year	Net profit
3	$1,525,000
4	1,892,000
5	2,303,000

Assuming the company went public in year four, the following chart shows the net profit that would be required in year four to enable management to earn its full 48.8% ownership participation at different price-earnings multiples:

Multiple	Net profit required ($000)
8 times	$2,187
9	1,944
10	1,750
12	1,458
15	1,167

Under this arrangement, management would receive its full percentage earn-out if it achieved its fourth-year projections and the stock sold at 9.3 multiple. Looking at the earn-out a little differently, if the company's stock sold at a multiple of 12 times earnings in the fourth year, management would have to earn approximately 77% of its projections to earn the full percentage.

Example 2 involves a company that was in existence, had a capital structure, was already publicly held, but was not profitable when the investment was completed. Its prospects appeared good, though. A reasonable deal was worked out, but not until a number of problems had been resolved.

The market price of the stock was about $8 at the time of negotiations. The problems were whether or not the company would make the profits it projected over the next two years and whether or not the marketplace would recognize these profits in terms of a healthy price-earnings multiple. The company wanted to convert subordinated debt into common stock as soon as possible to improve the balance sheet. The solutions were evolved through the use of a sliding scale in the exercise price of warrants. At the same time, though, investors gained the protection of a market price provision that must be met if the sliding scale prices are to be effective. This was further modified by establishing minimum earnings levels between those anticipated by management and those anticipated by the investors.

While this situation required a simpler capital structure than the case in Example 1, the needs of both management and venturer had been resolved satisfactorily.

1. Investment
   $3,700,000 (8½% subordinated note payable in years four through seven)
2. Warrant
   To purchase 518,260 shares of the company's common stock; the warrant exercise price per share is calculated as follows:
   a. Basic exercise price
      1) Years 1–3 $6.50 per share
      2) Years 4–5 $7.75 per share
      3) Years 6–7 $9.00 per share
   b. Effectiveness of basic exercise price

1) Years 4–5: common stock must be valued at least at $15.50 per share at the end of the third year; otherwise, the exercise price is $6.50 per share.
2) Years 6–7: common stock must be valued at least at $18.00 per share at the end of the fifth year, otherwise, the exercise price is $7.75 per share.

c. Exercise price modification for earnings
  1) If earnings are less than $.20 per share for the first year, the exercise price shall be $4.00 per share.
  2) If earnings are less than $.40 per share for the second year, the exercise price shall be $4.00 per share.
  3) If earnings are less than $.20 per share for the first year but more than $.40 per share for the second year, the exercise price shall be $5.25 per share.

Example 3 created particular problems for the venture capitalist. This situation represents third-round financing for a profitable company that needed significant money for additional expansion, beyond amounts that would be available from senior sources. A majority of this company's equity is controlled by one individual. The entrepreneur thought he might want to go public, and he was willing to give up some share of the business to develop a partner-like relationship with the venture capitalist in order to obtain the needed funds. However, he could have changed his mind for any number of reasons.

Since the company is controlled by the entrepreneur, our firm did not want to be a common stockholder under any circumstances short of holding liquid, nonrestricted securities. The structure adopted was a subordinated loan with warrants to purchase a convertible preferred stock. The loan was fully subordinated and carried an 8% interest rate.

We agreed that the investment called for a 10% equity participation. We also agreed that if the company went public in the next five years, our warrant would be exercisable only into common stock. However, if the company had not provided a public market at the end of five years, we could convert the balance of the subordinated note into preferred stock, which carries a high dividend rate (10% in nondeductible expense). Even though 10% is a high rate for a nondeductible expense, the actual $20,000 in dividends was small in relation to the anticipated profits. There was a specific reason for setting the dividend rate high: If the company had not provided the expected public market it was felt that the investor was entitled to a high current return to compensate for the long holding period of the investment and the risks incurred. In this example the investor was a corporation, which meant that dividends were subject to the 85% dividend received credit (100% credit for an SBIC).

1. Investment
   $400,000 (8% subordinated note payable in years four through seven)
2. Warrant
   To buy a 10% cumulative, convertible preferred stock
   a. Exercise price: $200,000
   b. Not exercisable into convertible preferred stock before the end of the fifth year
   c. If a public market is established prior to the warrant's being exercised into preferred stock, the warrant is exercisable *only* into common stock
   d. Expiration date: 10 years
3. Terms of convertible preferred
   a. Convertible at par at any time, into 10% of the company's common stock
   b. The holder is required to convert into common stock if a public market is established
   c. Put: the holder can put the convertible preferred to the company any time after the seventh year at a price of $400,000, as long as net worth is at least four times the put price just before the exercise of the put
   d. Call: the company can call the convertible preferred on 30 days' notice after the seventh year at the following prices:

Year	Call Price
8	$1,000,000
9	900,000
10	800,000
11	700,000
12	600,000
13 and thereafter	500,000

Liquidity

This still leaves the liquidity question: How do we get our money out of the situation if management changes its plan? A put-and-call arrangement was the solution. If the company built net worth of $1.6 million, the stock could be put to the company for $400,000 (cost basis was $200,000). At the same time, the investors provide management with a call at a high price in the eighth to thirteenth years of business. This protects us, the venture capitalists, from being bought out just before a public offering, in the event the company is successful. The call price declines with each passing year.

You might note that we were willing to accept a lower rate of return on the investment (smaller percentage of equity for a given amount invested) in Example 3, as compared to Examples 1 and 2. Our assessment indicated that the downside risk is less in this case than it is in new ventures or in companies running in the red.

Each situation in these three examples has its own peculiarities, each carries different assessments of risks and rewards, and there are any number of structuring and pricing possibliities that can be applied to take these differences into consideration. The needs of both the entrepreneur and the investor must be coordinated if a successful financing arrangement is to be negotiated. Generally, there is always some reasonable way to meet the needs of both in an attractive project.

PRICING

Pricing refers to the total return expected to be received over the life of the investment and includes both current income (interest and dividends) and the capital gains. The common denominator used is the valuation of the business—a $500,000 investment that receives 25% of the equity of the business values the company at $2 million (25% × $2 million = $500,000).

Arriving at a price for any investment is a matter of negotiation between the parties. This section will examine some of the considerations involved in setting a price, and methods for reducing some of the subjectivity of pricing from the perspective of the venture capitalist.

How Venture Capitalists Think about Pricing

The variable ingredients that go into price determinations are covered in the following questions:

1. How much money is the entrepreneur putting up relative to the total funds initially required?
2. What is the total in equity financing needed to launch the business? Or, conversely, how much additional dilution over the years will be necessary to keep the business moving forward at the desired pace?
3. How attractive will the company and industry be in the stock market, and what kind of price-earnings multiple will it be able to command in the marketplace now and in the years when the investors become interested in liquidating?
4. What is the upside potential of the investment; that is, how much in profits can be generated and in what period of time? What are the odds that the earnings and time projections can be met?
5. What is the downside potential; that is, what percentage of the total investment is likely to be lost if the project does not progress as anticipated? What are the odds that a loss will occur?

These considerations are directly related to many of the key issues discussed in other parts of this text concerning the cash flow of the business; how much lead time is needed before new products are accepted by the marketplace or by key customers; what it takes to educate a new market; how much has to be invested to carry losses while the operation is building up; what equity investments will be required to carry receivables, inventories, build new plants, and so forth; and how much the business can expect to borrow from conventional lenders and whether such financing will entail equity rights.

Profit Targets Set by Venture Firms

It is also important to keep in mind that venture capitalists have different profit targets. In fact, different investors could and do have different ideas of the appropriate expected rate of return for the same investment. For example, if a venture capitalist wants a return of four times his money in four years, the compound annual rate of return would be 41%. To illustrate rates of return, the following table has been prepared:

Profit Targets of Venture Capitalist	Compounded Annual Rates of Return (pre-tax)
Triple their money in three years	44%
Triple their money in five years	25%
Four times their money in four years	41%
Five times their money in three years	71%
Five times their money in five years	38%
Seven times their money in three years	91%
Seven times their money in five years	48%
Ten times their money in three years	115%
Ten times their money in five years	58%

These are internal rates of return. As a general rule, if venture capitalists are financing startups or first-stage projects, they are looking for expected returns at the high end of the scale. Thus, these investors would be looking for 40%, 50% or more compounded return on their investment. On the other hand, investors in second-stage financings tend to be looking for a 30% to 40% return per year and those making third-stage deals generally seek 25% to 30% per year.

In reviewing venture capitalists' pricing attitudes it is important also to keep in mind certain other things that have been repeated often throughout this text.

1. Nothing progresses along the originally projected pathway. (Murphy's Law stated another way: if things can go wrong, they will.) This is one of the world's more unpredictable activities, thus venture capitalists leave a great deal of room for such errors in arriving at valuations.
2. It is likely to take more money to accomplish objectives than indicated in projections by both management and venture analysts. Thus, venture capitalists like to leave room in the pricing for more dilution than might otherwise be expected.
3. It is difficult to realize profits on venture investments. Shares

received are not readily tradable as marketable securities. Instead, they must be sold under special rules established by SEC (Rule 144 stock sales), or they must be sold pursuant to the expensive and somewhat unpredictable action of obtaining a registration statement. The complications and obstacles involved in both of these alternatives are described by others in this text. The third alternative is to sell the entire business to a large listed company. This is also a complicated procedure and requires cooperation by all parties involved.

Obviously it is erroneous to assume that venture capitalists can use yardsticks like those used by regular security analysts in arriving at a fair valuation for their investment in the company.

Calculations Used by Venture Firms in Setting Price

On the other hand, some of the security analyst's tools are used in setting guidelines for valuation. The venture capitalist is likely to make a list of the various companies that are in the same industry as the firm requesting financing. Such a list will include industry leaders, medium-sized companies, and small firms. Key operating statistics for each company are likely to be compared; these include sales, operating costs, profits and margins, overhead and administrative expense, and net profit and its ratio to sales. Net worth and return on equity will also be calculated, together with long-term debt and current ratios. Price-earnings ratios in the current market are likely to be compared with an average worked out for the different classes of companies. If stocks of the leading firms are selling at 25 times earnings, medium companies at 15 times, and small companies eight times, there will certainly be a hesitancy to consider a price-earnings ratio of more than 10 to 12 in estimating what the venture equity could be worth at the time of sale.

To further illustrate this thinking, let us assume that the financing situation will be as follows. A company makes a medical instrument that has major potential for treatment of a serious disease. An analysis shows that the stocks of leading medical instrument companies are selling at 30 times earnings, medium firms at 20 times earnings, and small companies at 12 times earnings. Assume that the company seeking financing has current sales of $750,000 and is losing money, but evaluated projections by a venture capitalist indicate that in five years, sales will be $7.5 million and earnings $600,000 after taxes. (The entrepreneur's projections might have been $12 million in sales and $1 million in after-tax earnings.) Key questions about management, marketing, finance, etc. have been satisfactorily answered.

The venture capitalist might assume that in five years he will be able to liquidate his holdings on the basis of the company's being valued in the marketplace at $7.8 million (13 times earnings). He feels that this investment should produce a 44% compounded return on capital. Analysis indicates that it will take an initial investment of $500,000 to accomplish the five-year plan of the company. (The venture capitalist might also have to calculate a dilution factor if additional capital will be required.) Calculating the present value of the $500,000 investment for the five years using a 44% annual compounded growth rate factor, the $500,000 investment must have a value of $3,205,000 at the end of the fifth year. Assuming that the company will have a value of $7.8 million by that date (earnings of $60,000 times a multiple of 13), he would then require an initial 41.09% equity interest for his investment.

There are many variables. Will the venture capitalist really use a price-earnings multiple of 13 to calculate his value at the end of five years? This factor often depends on the state of the stock market. In good times, the venture capitalist might well use such a calculation, but during down markets, a price-earnings multiple of 10 or less is more likely. The difference has a major bearing on the equity percentage he will want for his $500,000. How accurate will the projections be? Will the company really be able to get by with only $500,000 in equity, despite the fact that it will grow from $750,000 to $7.8 million in five years, an average growth per year of 58% compounded?

These are only a few of the questions that the venture capitalist would ask himself in pondering the return he wants on his investment and the price to pay for the equity position.

The Pricing of Startups

In the case of startups, the pricing question becomes considerably more obscure. While the venture capitalist may go through a similar calculation, the returns expected are likely to be much higher than they are in the above illustration; thus, the investment will require a greater percentage of equity. Naturally the factors of unpredictability are much greater.

As a rough rule of thumb, if the venture capitalists are putting up all of the capital in a startup venture, they will probably want voting control of the venture. As described above, they might also include an earn-out program in the investment so that if certain prescribed targets are met, the entrepreneurs will be able to "earn" increasing amounts of equity. On the other hand, over the years some notable investments have been made where venture capitalists receive only 33% to 45% of equity after putting up all the capital. However, such transactions were generally worked out during strong stock markets with companies whose management represented some of the nation's leading executives in a "hot" industry.

Naturally, the greater the amount that the entrepreneur can invest, the less equity will be requested by the venture capitalist. For example, if the entrepreneur is putting up 30% of the capital, the venture firm might require only a 40% equity interest. Obviously these questions relate directly to key factors such as potential, quality, and risk. It should be noted that venture capitalists generally want the entrepreneur and his team to retain sufficient equity interests to ensure that they will be properly motivated. At the same time, if initial members of the management team are found to be inadequate or if they decide to leave, many venture capitalists will want to provide for a practical way to retire a portion of their initial stock interests.

How the Stock Market Affects Pricing

There is a direct relationship between venture pricing and the overall condition of the securities market. When the stock market is high and speculative stocks are quite popular, pricing will be quite different than it is during a down period when venture capital is more difficult to obtain and prices of small, speculative securities are quite low. While such conditions do not affect the pricing of startups as much as ongoing businesses, obviously the best time to raise money is when the stock market is strong and speculative fever is high.

The most astute entrepreneurs and managers will attempt to time their money-raising forays during these periods and then use debt during the down periods to implement the cash flow of the business, but these are highly unpredictable periods, and luck is as important as brains in raising capital during such periods.

During good times, venture capitalists generally feel that public offerings are the best way out of their investments. They are more generous with assumptions about price-earnings multiples than they are during a period like the 1973 liquidity crisis in the over-the-counter market, when it was virtually impossible to float a new issue and prices of small OTC stocks were exceedingly depressed.

Double-Check Values with the Venture Firms

There are ways to double-check pricing and valuation questions. Since most entrepreneurs will talk to various capital sources, they should compare the investors' suggestions on reasonable valuation. If three or four venture firms tend to agree on the equity percentage for a given investment, the entrepreneur should have more than adequate proof. Counsel with such intermediaries as accountants, lawyers, special consultants, investment bankers, and others can also help the entrepreneur decide what is the reasonable value of his company.

To transfer some of the qualitative assumptions about an investment into quantitative terms, the following model was developed while the author was at First Chicago Corporation. It can be a useful tool, but it is only a tool. None of the methods discussed in necessarily right or wrong generally or in a given situation.

XYZ Corporation is placing $300,000 in 7% convertible debentures. The company has been in existence for several years. The current year's operations will result in breaking even at $1,800,000 in sales. The product involves a high degree of technology. Four-year projections of sales and earnings are as follows (figures are in thousands).

Year	1	2	3	4
Sales	$2,800	$4,300	$6,300	$9,200
Net earnings				
Before tax	420	890	1,300	1,900
After tax	210	445	650	950

Structuring and Pricing the Financing /151

The problem is to determine what percentage of equity would be fair compensation for investing $300,000 in XYZ Corporation. It should be pointed out that there are three pricing methods compared in this illustration, described as traditional method, fundamental method, and The First Chicago Model.

Traditional Pricing Approach

Assumptions

1. Basic profit criterion is five times invested funds in four years, i.e., 50% compounded return on investment.
2. No explicit adjustment for risk.
3. Price-earnings ratio of 15 in Year 4.

Calculation

1. Year 4 net after-tax earnings are $950,000; therefore, total value of XYZ Corporation in Year 4 is $950,000 × 15 = $14,250,000
2. Desired value of investor's position in Year 4 is $300,000 × 5 = $1,500,000 + $300,000 = $1,800,000
3. Percentage of equity required is $1,800,000 ÷ $14,250,000 = 12.6%

Fundamental Pricing Method

The basic premise is that a venture investor ought to receive 20% or more, compounded annually, on all invested funds; therefore, the percentage of the company's equity accruing to the venture investor should equal the sum of the compounded earnings on the new investment divided by the total pre-tax projected earnings for the company over an equivalent period of time.

The earnings on $300,000 at various compounded rates over four years are as follows (figures are in thousands).

Rate	1	2	3	4	Total
20%	60	72	86	104	322
30%	90	117	152	198	557
40%	120	168	235	329	852

Dividing each of the totals (less interest received) by XYZ Corporation's four-year cumulative pre-tax projected profits of $4,510,000 produces the following percentages of equity required.

$$(322 - 81) \div 4,510 = 5.3\%$$
$$(557 - 81) \div 4,510 = 10.6\%$$
$$(852 - 81) \div 4,510 = 17.1\%$$

First Chicago Pricing Model

There are three basic directions a venture situation can take.

1. Successful: profitable to the point of being a solid public company
2. Sideways: marginally profitably with limited growth—not a viable public company but able to service debt over a period of years
3. Failure: bankruptcy or reorganization

Cash Flow for the Successful Investment
The cash flow to the investor if the company is quite successful might look like this (assume capital gains are realized in Year 4; figures are in thousands).

Year	1	2	3	4	5	6	7
Principal	0	0	0	0	0	0	0
Interest	21	21	21	18	0	0	0
Capital gain	0	0	0	X	0	0	0

Cash Flow for the Sideways Investment
The cash flow to the investor would be different, however, if the company became a limited growth situation (figures are in thousands).

Year	1	2	3	4	5	6	7
Principal	0	0	0	75	75	75	75
Interest	21	21	21	18	13	8	3
Capital gain	0	0	0	0	0	0	0

Cash Flow for the Failure Investment

If, unfortunately, the investment turned out to be a disaster, the cash flow might follow this pattern (assume a 10% recovery in Year 2; figures are in thousands).

Year	1	2	3	4	5	6	7
Principal	0	30	0	0	0	0	0
Interest	21	0	0	0	0	0	0
Capital gain	0	0	0	0	0	0	0

Compared Cash Flows

Comparing the cash flows for each of the three directions a venture investment might take produces the following (figures are in thousands).

Year	1	2	3	4	5	6	7
Sucessful ↑	21	21	21	18+X	0	0	0
Sideways →	21	21	21	93	88	83	78
Failure ↓	21	30	0	0	0	0	0

Probability Selection

The next step in this method involves assigning probabilities (P) to each of the three possible directions. The sum of these probabilities must, of course, equal 1.0. For the purposes of this example, we have chosen the following probabilities, but each type of project might well receive different weighting for probabilities of success and failure.

$$P \uparrow = .3 \text{ (3 chances in 10)}$$
$$P \rightarrow = .5 \text{ (5 chances in 10)}$$
$$P \downarrow = .2 \text{ (2 chances in 10)}$$
$$\overline{1.0}$$

Total Pricing Layout

After having selected an appropriate discount factor (for the entire portfolio), the overall layout is as follows (we have assumed an annual 20% compounded target portfolio return; figures are in thousands).

Discounted value of dollar	.83	.69	.58	.48	.40	.33	.28
Year	1	2	3	4	5	6	7
P ↑ .3	21	21	21	18+X	0	0	0
P → .5	21	21	21	93	88	83	78
P ↓ .2	21	30	0	0	0	0	0

Reduction to Present Value Equivalents

The next step is to reduce these numbers to their present value equivalents by multiplying them by the discount factor at the head of the column.

Year	1	2	3	4	5	6	7
P ↑ .3	17	15	12	9+.48X	0	0	0
P → .5	17	15	12	45	35	27	22
P ↓ .2	17	21	0	0	0	0	0

Pricing Equation

We now total each row and then construct the basic equation that will provide the desired output.

Probability	Row total
P ↑ .3	53 + .48X
P → .5	173
P ↓ .2	38

$$300 = P(\uparrow)(53) + .48X) + P(\rightarrow) 173 + P(\downarrow) 38$$

Using the probabilities shown above.

$$300 = (.3)(53 + .48X) + (.5)(173) + (.2)(38)$$

Decision Matrix

				Percentage of firm needed at		
P1	P2	P3	X	P/E 10	P/E 15	P/E 30
0.8	0.0	0.2	648.0	6.8	4.5	2.3
0.7	0.1	0.2	704.7	7.4	4.9	2.5
0.6	0.2	0.2	780.3	8.2	5.5	2.7
0.5	0.3	0.2	886.1	9.3	6.2	3.1
0.4	0.4	0.2	1,044.9	11.0	7.3	3.7
→ 0.3	**0.5**	**0.2 ← 1,309.5**		**13.8**	**9.2**	**4.6**
0.2	0.6	0.2	1,838.7	19.4	12.9	6.5
0.1	0.7	0.2	3,426.2	36.1	24.0	12.0

The row set in bold type shows the present value of $300,000 if a 20% compound growth rate is to be achieved, based on different probability assumptions shown on each line. The line marked ← → shows the assumptions given in this problem about success, or sideways movement of the investment.

Thus, if a price-earnings multiple of 15 is to be used to calculate the value of the company, a 9.2% equity will be required to achieve the compound growth rate of 20%, given the probability requirements in the example. The columns headed P/E 10 and P/E 30 show the percentage of equity needed under those price-earnings multiples.

Comparison of Three Pricing Methods

The percentage of equity required under the three pricing methods is as follows: traditional, 12.9%, fundamental, 5.3%; First Chicago, 9.2%.

Effect of Varying the Interest Rate

What happens if the interest rate on the debenture is doubled, from 7% to 14%, for example?

| | | | | Percentage of firm needed at | | |
P1	P2	P3	X	P/E 10	P/E 15	P/E 30
0.8	0.0	0.2	529.2	5.6	3.7	1.9
0.7	0.1	0.2	566.3	6.0	4.0	2.0
0.6	0.2	0.2	615.9	6.5	4.3	2.2
0.5	0.3	0.2	685.2	7.2	4.8	2.4
0.4	0.4	0.2	789.2	8.3	5.5	2.8
0.3	**0.5**	**0.2**	**982.5**	**10.1**	**6.8**	**3.4**
0.2	0.6	0.2	1,369.1	13.8	9.2	4.6
0.1	0.7	0.2	2,348.9	24.7	16.5	8.2

This table shows that the equity percentage required on the investment will drop from 9.2% to 6.8% and still produce the same return to First Chicago if the interest rate on the debenture doubles, from 7% to 14%.

Effect of Varying the Time Horizon

What is the effect of pushing out the realization of capital gains to Year 7?

| | | | | Percentage of firm needed at | | |
P1	P2	P3	X	P/E 10	P/E 15	P/E 30
0.8	0.0	0.2	1,119.7	11.8	7.9	3.9
0.7	0.1	0.2	1,217.7	12.8	8.5	4.3
0.6	0.2	0.2	1,348.4	14.2	9.5	4.7
0.5	0.3	0.2	1,531.2	16.1	10.7	5.4
0.4	0.4	0.2	1,805.6	19.0	12.7	6.3
0.3	**0.5**	**0.2**	**2,262.8**	**23.8**	**15.9**	**7.9**
0.2	0.6	0.2	3,177.2	33.4	22.3	11.1
0.1	0.7	0.2	5,920.5	62.3	41.5	20.8

This table shows the effects of moving the realization of capital gains from the fourth to the seventh year, keeping all other assumptions the same. The investment now will require a 15.9% equity interest rather than 9.2%.

Legal Documents of Venture Financing

ROBERT R. MAC DONALD and RICHARD J. TESTA, ESQ.

The purpose of this article is to familiarize the entrepreneur with the legal documents he is likely to encounter in the closing of a venture financing. These documents are typically long and complex, but all deserve close scrutiny because they establish the ongoing rights and responsibilities of the parties to the financing.

After an informal agreement is reached on the principal terms of the financing, it is the investor's prerogative to have his lawyer prepare the legal documents. Although the bulk of the documents will cover relatively conventional ground, there will be areas for negotiation. These areas can be ferreted out by counsel experienced in the private placement area. Counsel inexperienced in venture financings may find fault with points that are standard practice in venture financings.

Although it is unlikely that an aggressive negotiating approach by the entrepreneur will "sour" the deal, it should be noted that these initial negotiations do establish the tone for ongoing, working relationships. The entrepreneur should use his lawyer's advice and his own judgment to determine a negotiating posture.

Various documents and provisions that may be used for a venture financing are discussed below. Any particular financing would require deletions and additions; therefore, the entrepreneur should work closely with his attorney to make sure the documents are applicable and complete for his financing.

PURCHASE AGREEMENT

The basic document of venture capital financing is the purchase agreement. Other agreements are usually mentioned in the purchase agreement and are then either appended to it or circulated as separate documents. The purchase agreement usually includes the sections discussed below, but the venture capitalist will tailor the agreement from the provisions listed in the sections.

The purchase agreement is structured to accomplish three main objectives:

1. To serve as a disclosure document to give the investor a detailed view of various legal and financial aspects of the company he is investing in;
2. To set forth various conditions with respect to which the investor must be satisfied before he makes the investment; and
3. To set forth various agreements between the investor and the entrepreneur/company relating to the ongoing operation of the company and the ongoing relationship between the investor and the entrepreneur/company. This is necessary because typically no single investor assumes control over the company. SBICs are prohibited from initially assuming control.

The disclosure objective is accomplished through the "representations and warranties" section of the purchase agreement. The conditions to closing are contained in a separate section of the purchase agreement. The ongoing relationships are spelled out in a section or sections relating to "covenants" of the company and other ancillary agreements such as a stock restriction agreement. The typical sections of a purchase agreement are discussed in more detail below.

Section I. Description of the Financing

1. *Authorization:* The company states that the securities to be issued have been properly authorized. The securities are de-

scribed briefly, and, if the investor is acquiring a note (whether or not convertible) or a stock purchase warrant, reference will be made to the form of the security, which will be attached as an exhibit to the purchase agreement. If the investor is acquiring preferred stock, the terms of the preferred stock (which must ultimately be reflected in any amendment to the corporate charter) may be outlined in a term sheet attached to the purchase agreement as an exhibit.
2. *Sale and purchase of securities:* The company agrees to sell the securities, and the purchaser agrees to buy them at the specified price. The time and place of the closing are specified, and various terms of the exchange are enumerated.
3. *Other participants:* Other participants in the financing may be listed or referenced, and the point may be made that identical purchase agreements are being executed simultaneously with the other participants. A condition of the investor's obligation to purchase may be that all other agreements have not been amended and are in full force on the closing date.
4. *Use of proceeds:* Restrictions on the use of the proceeds can be enumerated, or reference may be made to a specific investment schedule.

Section II. Representations and Warranties of the Company

The lengthy documentation of venture financings performs a vital function in obtaining detailed disclosure of material financial and legal information about the venture company. This function is as important as that of establishing rights and remedies in the event of default or misrepresentation. Included in the list of representations and warranties are those items that the purchaser has relied on in making his investment decision and whose accuracy the company is in a postion to verify. The company must review these representations and warranties extremely carefully because any misrepresentation or breach of warranty may give the investor rights to damages or even to rescind the entire transaction.

As noted above, the section on representations and warranties, like the other sections, will be drafted with the investor's viewpoint in mind. The lawyer doing the drafting, who will be largely unfamiliar with the company, will make the *assumption* that the company is totally "clean" and may draft page after page of detailed representations and warranties to this effect. The entrepreneur should not be alarmed at this. Although the investor will expect that major legal and financial problems have already been disclosed to him at this point, he will also expect that there are some minor "skeletons in the closet." The fact that a representation in the first draft is not true does not mean that the investor will want to back out of the deal. What the investor is looking for and what the entrepreneur is expected to provide is a detailed disclosure of what the business is like at a given point in time—a balance sheet approach. If any representation is not correct the investor and his lawyer should be informed so the document can be revised. The entrepreneur is expected to represent only what he should know about his company, and the principal points of negotiation in the representations and warranties section are to limit the representations to non-trivial areas and to areas reasonably within the knowledge of the entrepreneur.

A list of typical venture financing representations and warranties follows:

1. *Organization and corporate power:* Statement that the company is duly organized, is in good standing, and is qualified to do business in all appropriate jurisdictions.
2. *Subsidiaries:* Description of any subsidiaries and any investments in the securities of any other firm.
3. *Business:* Description of the business in which the company is engaged and/or intends to engage.
4. *Authorization:* Statement that the company will be bound by the agreement and that execution of the agreement has been duly authorized by all necessary actions of the company.
5. *Capitalization:* Description of the company's authorized capitalization and status of the company's outstanding securities, including warrants, options, and convertible securities. In addition, any transfer restrictions, repurchase rights, preemptive rights, will be described.
6. *Financial statements:* Statement that audited and interim financial statements are accurate and complete and have been prepared in accordance with generally accepted accounting

principles. Specifics, such as method of inventory valuation and status of accounts receivable, may be included.

7. *Absence of undisclosed liabilities:* Statement that, except as disclosed or reserved against on the balance sheet, there are no material undisclosed claims, encumbrances, or liabilities.
8. *Absence of certain developments:* Affirmation that there have been no material adverse changes since the date of the last balance sheet. A detailed listing could include such items as no dividends or other distributions, no loss of property, no labor trouble, no change in assets, and no condition that constitutes an event of default (as defined elsewhere).
9. *Offering circular:* Statement that the offering circular used by the company in seeking the financing was accurate and complete.
10. *Title to properties:* Affirmation that the company has good and marketable title to all of its properties and assets. An exhibit will normally list any real property owned or leased by the company and any liens, restrictions, or encumbrances on such property. Assurance that the company has necessary property and assets to conduct its business as presently conducted and that they are in good condition and adequately insured.
11. *Applicable statutes:* Statement that the company is in compliance with applicable statutes, regulations, and rules necessary to do business.
12. *Tax matters:* Statement that all tax returns have been duly filed and that taxes have been paid or provision has been made on the latest balance sheet.
13. *Contracts and commitments:* All material contracts and commitments will ordinarily be listed in an exhibit to the purchase agreement. These may include employment contracts, stock agreements, financing agreements, licenses, leases, pension plans, or stock option plans. Statement that the company is not in default under any contract and that no contract will have a material adverse effect on the business.
14. *Patents:* Statement that the company holds the necessary patents, trademarks, and copyrights to conduct its business, and that to the best of its knowledge it does not infringe patents, trademarks, or copyrights of others. Patents and

similar proprietary rights may be specifically identified in an exhibit to the purchase agreement.
15. *Effect of transactions:* Statement that the execution, delivery, and performance of the purchase agreement and the issuance and delivery of the securities being acquired by the investor will not conflict with or result in any violation or breach or any default under any other obligations of the company; that transactions do not violate any statutes or regulations or the corporate charter of the company.
16. *Litigation:* Declaration that there is no litigation, suit, claim or governmental investigation pending or, to the company's knowledge, threatened against the company.
17. *Other agreements with principals:* Declaration that there are no material undisclosed agreements with, or obligations to, principals.
18. *Insider agreements:* Disclosure of material contracts and commitments between company and stockholders or officers.
19. *Offerees:* Statement that the issuance of the securities will qualify as a private placement under the Securities Act of 1933. There may be a statement concerning the sophistication of offerees.
20. *Corporate charter and bylaws:* Statement that the investor has been furnished with copies of the corporate charter and bylaws, as amended to date. If such amendments have been made, the documents may be appended to the purchase agreement.
21. *Brokerage:* Description of any finder's fee or broker's fee or commission payable in connection with the financing.
22. *Disclosure:* Declaration that no document, certificate, or statement furnished by the company in connection with this financing contains any untrue statement of a material fact or omits to state a material fact necessary in order to make the statement not misleading and that all facts have been disclosed that would materially adversely affect the business.

Section III. Representations of the Purchaser

This section is short and usually has only two purposes. The first is to represent that the purchaser has full power and authority to perform the agreement in accordance with its terms. The second is to establish that the transaction qualifies as a private placement. For this purpose the purchaser represents that he is purchasing the securities for investment and not with an intent to sell or distribute them. He also represents that he considers himself to be a sophisticated investor, that he has made detailed inquiry concerning the company, and that the officers have made available all information requested by the purchaser.

Section IV. Conditions Precedent to Closing

The purchase agreement normally specifies certain conditions to the purchaser's obligation; occasionally there is, in addition, a separate section detailing conditions to the seller's obligation.

Unless the purchase agreement is signed before the closing takes place, there is technically no need for a conditions section—the purchase agreement is simply not signed until the deal is ready to close. Generally deferred closings do not take place in venture financing situations, but the agreement may be signed up if some future event (such as delivery of audited year-end financials) must take place before the closing, and the parties wish to "lock up" the deal. In either case, for convenience, the purchase agreement is drafted *as if* there will be a deferred closing and specifies the following typical conditions which must be satisfied before the investor will close the deal.

1. *Opinion of counsel for the company:* A favorable opinion from counsel for the company covering the proper execution and the binding nature of the various agreements, the good standing of the company, the capitalization of the company, the absence of litigation, the absence of violations in contracts or in the company's charter, the conformance with applicable state blue sky and federal securities laws, and other requested items. The purpose of this requirement is to give the investor the "comfort" of knowing that an independent party familiar with the company has reviewed all important legal matters.

2. *Opinion of counsel for the purchasers:* Counsel for the investor supplies a favorable written opinion dated the closing date and covering the same basic points as those received from the

company's counsel. He may rely on certain opinions provided to him by counsel for the company.
3. *Representations and warranties:* Certification that the representations and warranties made by the company are true and correct on the closing date.
4. *Performance:* Assurance that the company shall have conformed and complied with all of the agreements and conditions prior to closing.
5. *No event of default:* Assurance that, if there are any default provisions in the agreements, there shall exist at the closing date no event or act that constitutes default or will lead to default. This provision would be included only in deals in which debt was issued.
6. *Other agreements:* Statement that any important credit or loan or other agreements have been effected.
7. *Other purchase agreements:* Statement that the agreements of all other participants in the financing have been signed and payment tendered for a specified minimum number of shares or amount of money. This provision is important when there is more than one investor, so that if any investor backs out, the others can restructure the deal.
8. *Compliance certificate:* Statement that the purchasers will receive at the closing a certificate signed by the president and treasurer certifying that the conditions specified in the preceding paragraphs have been fulfilled.
9. *Other provisions:* Provision for execution of employment contracts and stock restriction agreements, receipt of revised financial statements, resignation of specific directors or officers, payment of all amounts owed to the company by officers and directors, or anything else peculiar to the particular deal which must be effected before the investor purchases the securities.

Section V. Covenants of the Company

The covenants describe the continuing obligations of the company to the purchaser with respect to future actions of the company. This section often is presented under two headings to separate affirmative and negative covenants. Affirmative covenants are those positive actions the company promises to make, and negative covenants are actions or results that the company promises to avoid. The previous sections of the purchase agreement are in many respects standard—or boiler plate. This section is more often tailored to the individual deal.

In an equity-oriented venture capital investment, where the purchaser will control the board of directors, the covenants are often kept to a minimum. In such situations, the affirmative covenants might merely provide that the purchaser will receive periodic financial information and will be represented on the board. The negative covenants might limit only the company's ability to amend its corporate charter or merge or sell its assets without the purchaser's consent. A venture capital firm with board control will generally rely upon this to influence the direction of a company. Accordingly, it will not, as a rule, find it necessary to impose in advance extensive restrictions on the conduct of the business by insisting on strict affirmative and negative covenants. (Where the venture capital firm is acquiring securities which are debt-oriented and where there is no board control more extensive covenants are appropriate). Among the covenants which are found in venture capital purchase agreements are the following:

Affirmative Covenants
1. *Maintenance of corporate existence:* The company will maintain its corporate existence and all rights, licenses, patents, copyrights, trademarks, etc. useful in its business, and will engage only in the type of business described in the representations and warranties.
2. *Payment of taxes and claims:* The company will pay all lawful taxes, assessments, and levies upon the company or its income or property before they become in default. A separate covenant sometimes provides that principal and interest on any debt securities acquired by the purchaser will be paid when due.
3. *Legal compliance:* The company will comply with all applicable laws and regulations in the conduct of its business.
4. *Repair and maintenance:* The company will keep all necessary equipment and property in good repair and condition, as necessary to permit the business to be properly conducted.

5. *Property and liability insurance:* The company will maintain insurance against hazards and risks and liability to persons and property to the extent customary for corporations engaged in the same or a similar business.
6. *Life insurance:* The purchaser will often require the company to maintain insurance on the lives of key officers and employees. The face amount in some cases may be as much as the purchase amount of the securities, and the insurance proceeds are often payable directly to the purchaser, particularly if the purchaser holds debt securities.
7. *Employment contracts:* The company may covenant to enter into employment contracts with all key employees covering salary, nondisclosure of information during and after the term of employment, assignment of patents, and noncompetition for a specified period (often several years) after termination of employment.
8. *Accounts and reports:* The company may be asked by the purchaser to agree to maintain a standard system of accounting in accordance with generally accepted accounting principles consistently applied, and to keep full and complete financial records.
9. *Financial operating statements:* The company will generally agree to provide the investors with detailed financial and operating information. The information to be provided may include annual, quarterly, and sometimes monthly reports of sales, production, shipments, estimated profits, cash balances, receivables, payables, and backlog; all statements filed with the SEC or other agencies; and any other information that the investor may need for his own voluntary or involuntary filing requirements. The right to receive financial information is often terminated when the company goes public to avoid dissemination of "inside" information. A covenant may also establish preparation and approval procedures for budgets.
10. *Adverse change:* The company will advise the purchaser of any event—financial, legal or otherwise—that represents a material adverse change in the condition of the business.
11. *Current ratio, working capital, or net worth:* These covenants normally are included only in debt financings and are

agreements to maintain the current ratio, working capital, or net worth, either at a minimum amount or as specified for various time periods. They may be keyed to projections made by the company.
12. *Board of directors:* Venture capital firms will generally seek assurances that they will be represented on the company's board of directors. The right to be represented on the board may be backed up by stock voting agreements with the principal stockholders. If the investors are not to be represented on the board, the company may be required to notify the investor of the time and place of board meetings and to permit the investor or his representative to attend such meetings.
13. *Access to premises:* The investor or his representative will generally be permitted to make inspections of the company's property and books and records.
14. *Future financings:* The investor may be given the right of first refusal, or preemptive rights on any future financings.
15. *Use of proceeds:* The use of funds may be broadly stated in terms of the business of the company, or it may be narrowly defined to comply with a financing plan.
16. *Dealings with related parties:* The company covenants that all transactions between the company and stockholders of the company shall be conducted on an arm's length basis and shall be on terms no less favorable to the company than could be obtained from nonrelated persons.

Negative Covenants

1. *Nature of business:* The company agrees not to change the nature of the business from that described in the representations and warranties.
2. *Business entity:* The purchaser may, under certain circumstances, be able to compel the company to agree not to amend the corporate charter or bylaws without the consent of the purchaser. More narrowly drawn covenants might prohibit only certain specified actions (e.g., change of fiscal year or a change in the capital structure) without the purchaser's consent.
3. *Issuance of stock or convertible securities:* The investor may require the company not to issue any securities that would

result in dilution of the purchaser's position. This includes restrictions on issuance of securities of the type issued to the purchaser and any securities convertible into such securities at a price less than that paid by the purchaser.

4. *Redemption of securities:* The company may covenant not to repurchase or redeem any of its securities except in accordance with the terms of the particular securities, stock option plans, and agreements with the holders.
5. *Sale or purchase of assets, mergers, and consolidation:* Consolidations, mergers, acquisitions, and the like without the investor's advance approval are often prohibited. Liquidation and dissolution of the company and the sale, lease, or other disposition of substantial assets without consent may also be barred. Restrictions may also be placed on the company's purchase of capital assets.
6. *Liabilities assumed:* The purchase agreement may provide for restrictions on liens, pledges, and other encumbrances, with exceptions for such liabilities as real estate mortgages. Separate restrictions can be placed on leases of real property or equipment.
7. *Indebtedness:* The company may agree to restrictions on future indebtedness, with exceptions for institutional senior borrowings, indebtedness on personal property purchase money obligations and trade indebtedness, up to certain limits in the ordinary course of business.
8. *Investments:* Restrictions against making investments in any other companies may be imposed by the purchaser.
9. *Distributions:* The company frequently agrees not to make any dividend distributions to stockholders. Dividends may be eliminated until a given date or may be limited to a fixed percentage of profits above a set amount.
10. *Employee compensation:* The company may agree to limit employment and other personal service contracts to a maximum term and a maximum amount of annual compensation.
11. *Loans and advances:* Loans to stockholders and employees may be barred unless approved by the board of directors.
12. *Aging of payables:* The company may covenant not to allow accounts payable to exceed certain aging. Limitations can also be placed on assets or other liabilities. These covenants are normally seen only in debt-oriented investments.

13. *Default on agreements:* The company may expressly covenant not to default on this purchase agreement or any other agreement.

Section VI. Covenants of the Purchaser

Occasionally, the purchaser may agree at the time of the initial investment to participate in a second round of financing. The terms of such second-round financing, including the timing of the financing, the amount and type of securities to be acquired, and any conditions to the purchaser's obligation to participate in such financing, will be set forth in a separate section of the original purchase agreement.

Section VII. Registration Rights and Related Provisions Regarding Resale of Securities by the Purchase

The securities acquired by a venture capital firm are not registered under the Securities Act of 1933 at the time of issuance; instead, they are issued by the company pursuant to the "private placement" exemption from registration under that act. As privately issued, "restricted" securities, they can be resold only if they are subsequently registered under the act or an exemption from registration is available for the proposed resale. To maximize his ability to resell the securities, the purchaser typically negotiates with the company for the right to require the company to register the securities under certain circumstances. These registration rights will generally give the holder the unilateral right to "demand" registration of its securities as well as the right to "piggyback" its securities on any other registration of securities by the company. The following is a brief summary of typical provisions relating to registration rights:

1. *Demand registrations:* If permitted at all, the purchaser's right to demand registration will generally be limited in number and/or in time. Usually a holder or holders of only a stated percentage of the securities must request the registration.
2. *"Piggyback" rights:* Because piggyback registrations are less burdensome financially, the provisions regarding piggyback

registrations are generally more liberal than the demand registration provisions and will not, as a rule, be limited as to time or number. Piggyback rights are, however, often subject to the approval of the managing underwriter of the offering.
3. *Registrations on Form S-16:* If the company's stock is publicly traded and if certain other conditions are met, the company may be able to register the purchaser's stock on Form S-16, an inexpensive, abbreviated registration form. The company will often be asked to agree to register the purchaser's securities on Form S-16, if that form is available, without significant limits as to time or number.
4. *Allocation of expenses:* The purchase agreement may provide that the company will pay all future registration expenses or that the expenses will be allocated among the sellers. Often the company will agree to pay the expenses of one, or perhaps two, demand registrations, with the expenses of any subsequent demand registrations being borne by the sellers.
5. *Indemnification:* The company will generally agree to compensate and hold harmless the seller against any losses, claims, or damages that result from an untrue statement or a material omission by the company in any registration statement. The seller will also agree to indemnify the company if claims result from false statements or omissions by the seller.

As noted above, the purchaser's securities may be resold without registration if an exemption from registration is available. Rule 144, promulgated under the Securities Act of 1933, establishes ground rules for qualifying for an exemption. In order for the purchaser to be able to resell under Rule 144, the company's securities must be registered with the Securities and Exchange Commission under the Securities Exchange Act of 1934 (which should not be confused with the Securities Act of 1933), and the company must have filed certain reports required by that Act. Alternatively, certain information must be publicly available concerning the company. The purchaser may request the company, in the purchase agreement, to agree to register under the Securties Exchange Act of 1934 upon the demand of the purchaser. At a minimum, the purchaser will request that, should the company become subject to the reporting requirements of the 1934 Act, the company will take all action necessary to make Rule 144 available.

Section VIII. Miscellaneous

The following provisions are noncontroversial, boiler plate items:

1. *Survival of representations and warranties:* Statement that the representations and warranties made in connection with the transaction should be binding after the date of closing.
2. *Successors and assigns:* Assurance that the agreement shall bind and inure to the benefit of successors and assigns of the parties of the agreement, including any assignee of the purchaser who purchases any of the securities from the purchaser in a transaction exempt from registration.
3. *Notices:* List of addresses for communication among parties to the agreement.
4. *Expenses:* The company generally agrees to pay all out-of-pocket expenses arising in connection with the transaction. The purchaser may represent that he has not dealt with any broker or finder, or, if brokerage or finders fees are to be paid, such fees will be specified.
5. *Entire agreement:* Statement that the purchase agreement embodies the entire agreement and understanding between the purchaser and the company and supersedes all prior agreements and understandings relating to the subject matter of the agreement.
6. *Amendments and waivers:* Statement that terms and provisions of the purchase agreement cannot be modified except in a writing executed by the company and holders of a certain percentage of the securities, and a statement that a waiver by the investor of his rights under one provision shall not be considered a waiver of other rights.
7. *Counterparts:* Statement that the purchase agreement may be executed simultaneously in two or more counterparts, each of which is deemed an original, but all of which together constitute one and the same instrument.
8. *Governing law:* Designation of the state under whose laws the agreement is to be governed.

DESCRIPTION OF SECURITIES

A venture capital deal may involve any combination of debt, warrants, preferred stock, and common stock. The purchase agreement, as discussed above, usually presents the general terms of the agreement and is supplemented with the forms of the debentures or warrants, or a description of the terms of the preferred stock. It is possible for these forms to be only several pages in length if such items as restrictive covenants, events of default, and conversion privileges are covered in the purchase agreement.

If there are separate descriptions for common or preferred stock, the agreements would detail the specific class of stock and any dividend, voting, and conversion privileges of those shares. Likely provisions of debentures and warrants are given below.

DEBENTURES

The following are typical provisions found in debentures or notes:

1. *Description of the note:* This will include such items as the interest rate, the aggregate principal amount, and the date of maturity. If the notes are convertible, a section will be added covering the items discussed below under stock purchase warrants.
2. *Conditions of prepayment:* The notes may be prepaid according to a schedule that results in reduced prepayment penalities as the notes mature. Sometimes they can be prepaid without penalty as long as the prepayments are in specified minimum amounts and are made on specified payment dates.
3. *Collateral:* The note may be secured with common stock or with assets of the company.
4. *Subordination:* If the note is subordinated, the agreement will acknowledge subordination to certain forms of senior debt, including bank borrowings. Normally, debts to officers of the company will be subordinated to this debt.
5. *Covenants of the company:* This section may refer to the covenants in the purchase agreement or may elaborate on those covenants. When debt is a part of the purchase, the covenants

are normally more strict and include restrictions on the current ratio and net worth. These stricter covenants give the venture capitalist more bargaining power if the company develops problems.

6. *Default:* The events of default and the remedies upon default are enumerated. Possible events of default are:

    - Default in payment of installment of interest or principal
    - Default in payments on any other loans
    - Default in any covenants
    - False information in the agreement
    - Institution of bankruptcy proceedings
    - Nonpayment of court judgments

    The section on remedies upon default will state that the holders of more than a given percentage of the outstanding principal amount of notes can declare the principal and accrued interest due and payable. The holder of any note may proceed to protect and enforce his rights by legal action, and the company will reimburse the holder for all reasonable costs associated with enforcement of his rights.

7. *Waiver and amendment:* This provision states how many noteholders are required to amend the agreement, with the stipulation that payments due to an individual noteholder cannot be changed without his consent.

Stock Purchase Warrant Agreement

When a transaction includes stock purchase warrants, a form of warrant must be prepared which will set forth the terms of the warrant.

1. *Rights represented by warrant:* Statement that the rights may be exercised in whole or in part by surrender of the warrant and payment of the purchase price.
2. *Availability of shares:* Agreement of the company to authorize and have available for issue sufficient shares of stock for exercise of the warrants.

3. *Adjustments to exercise price:* This is normally a lengthy section and may include the following provisions:

   a. Statement of a formula for determining the reduction in warrant purchase price if common stock is sold for less than the warrant purchase price or less than the current market price.
   b. Statement that the warrant price is reduced by the value of dividends on the common stock.
   c. Statement of how the warrant price is adjusted for stock splits.
   d. Statement that, if any of the previous adjustments are made to the warrant purchase price, how an adjustment is made to the number of shares that can be purchased at the new warrant price.
   e. Statement that the company is not required to adjust for currently outstanding warrants and options.
   f. Assurance that the holder will receive proportional rights, given in writing, prior to reorganization, liquidation, consolidation, or merger.
   g. Statement that the holder will receive written notification of adjustments in the warrant price.

4. *Written notice:* Specification that the holders will receive written notice before declaration of a dividend, reorganization, merger, or liquidation.
5. *Definitions of common stock:* Statement that "common stock" is defined to include capital stock of any class that is not limited to a fixed sum or percentage in respect to participation in dividends or distributions of assets.
6. *Expiration date:* Specification of the last date for exercising the warrants.
7. *Transfer of warrants:* Specification that the warrants and all rights are transferable and negotiable.
8. *Exchange of warrants:* Statement that the warrants are exchangeable for new warrants representing the then existing exercise price and shares.

ANCILLARY AGREEMENTS

Mention was made in the discussion of the purchase agreement of supplemental information that would be appended to the purchase agreement. Some of this additional information is an innocuous as a list of the participants in the financing, additional information about the business of the company, and the purpose of the financing. Other agreements may be employment contracts, personal guarantees, and a restatement of certain key representations and warranties for which the investors want to hold the officers personally liable. The age and form of the venture dictate the type and form of ancillary agreements. The following agreements are examples.

Employment Agreements

These will stipulate that key employees agree to work for the company for a specified period of time, that they will not compete with the company for a specified number of years after leaving the company, and that they will not reveal confidential company information while employed by or after leaving the company. Such an agreement may also stipulate that the company is given the right to all discoveries, inventions, processes, etc., discovered or created while an employee is under employment, whether or not he is actually "on the job," so long as the inventions relate to areas of his work.

Previous Employment

In a startup venture, the investors want to make sure that the entrepreneurs are free from previous employment agreements and that prior employers do not intend and do not have grounds to take legal action against the entrepreneurs. Toward this end, there may be copies of prior employment agreements, statements from prior employers concerning the status of the entrepreneurs, and representations by the entrepreneurs that they have not revealed or transferred trade secrets or confidential information of previous employers and are not bound by any agreements with former employers, or otherwise restricted from participating full time in the company's business.

Stock Restriction Agreements

Investors may require that they be given a right of first refusal on all stock transactions by any officer, director, or key employee. As previously mentioned, the investors may also require that the principal stockholders agree to vote for the investors' nominees to the board of directors. The form of the stock restriction agreement will generally be attached to the purchase agreement as an exhibit.

DOCUMENTS THAT FORM A BASIS FOR INVESTMENT

Key documents that were used in evaluating the company will ofen be listed and described on an exhibit attached to the purchase agreement. These can include leases, title documents to patents or processes, development grants, purchase orders issued and received, licenses from regulatory bodies, and business plans. These documents will be made available to the investors and their counsel for inspection.

CONSULTING CONTRACT

Some investors may require the company to contract with the investor for financial and management consulting services. This type of consulting contract will usually be a brief document reciting a simple description of the services engaged and the terms and amount of payment to be made. Venture capitalists who play an active role in the management of their investments usually intend to provide these services without charge as a means of protecting their investment.

THE CLOSING PROCESS

After the parties have reached agreement on the terms of purchase agreement and the other documents which set forth the fundamental terms of the transaction, the parties may, as previously noted, elect to "lock up" the deal by executing the purchase agreement. In any event, counsel for both parties will at this stage review the proposed transaction and the records and proceedings of the company and will prepare opinions for delivery to the purchasers at the closing. Ancillary agreements will be finalized. Also, good standing certificates and tax status certificates will be obtained from appropriate government agencies. Other closing documents may include: the compliance certificate, signed by the company's president and treasurer indicating that all representations and warranties set forth in the purchase agreement are true and correct as of the closing date and that all conditions to closing have been satisfied; a "cold comfort" letter from the auditors stating that there are no material adverse changes; an incumbency and signature certificate listing the officers of the company and showing their signatures; the investment, or nondistribution, letters of the investors; and cross receipts acknowledging the transfer of securities and money.

Representatives of the investor, officers of the company, and counsel for both parties will generally be present at the closing. At the closing, the parties will deliver executed originals of the closing instruments and documents required by the purchase agreement. The sale is consummated when the company delivers the certificates representing the securities sold and receives from the purchaser the full purchase price of the securities.

Venture Capital in Practice: A Case History

TIMOTHY M. PENNINGTON

How does the venture capitalist actually make an investment decision? How does he put into practice the principles described in the other articles in this book?

The following is a case history of how an investment opportunity was pursued by our firm. Some information has been changed to conceal the identity of the specific situation. An important thought to keep in mind is that each investment opportunity is unique and has its own distinctive characteristics, therefore, details covered in this case history may not apply to other projects. Furthermore, situations will vary because venture capitalists have their own ideas of the relative importance of the various aspects of a business venture. Different venture groups, therefore, attach varying degrees of importance to the elements of a given investment opportunity. Also the key elements often vary between differing situations.

This is a case history of a startup project. The description does not include all of the investigation and analysis that was done, but highlights the most important aspects. The project involved four men in the 1930s with an idea. Working out of their homes, these four men had written a business plan and had developed a working prototype of the product they intended to exploit.

THE BUSINESS PLAN AND THE MANAGEMENT

Our firm started with a thorough reading of the business plan. The plan was extremely well formulated and written. This was an important positive factor because there were not many historical facts and figures to analyze in this startup venture. The product involved was a labor- and cost-saving electromechanical device. It didn't do anything in a revolutionary way, but it was an evolutionary improvement over existing products in terms of cost/performance. It was a "medium technology" device—meaning it utilized existing state-of-the-art knowledge and materials—and was not pushing any new frontiers of esoteric technology.

The company wanted to raise $500,000, which their projections showed would last until positive cash flow from operations was reached. This was one of the items that would need careful scrutiny because the amount of capital required is a pivotal element in all deals.

After becoming interested in the opportunity from reading the business plan, we had an initial meeting with the four men and discussed all aspects of the venture as a general overview. We asked for an extensive list of references for the men because the requirement of good management, very important in all deals, is even more critical in a startup. We spent a considerable amount of time telephoning these references. In addition to the references provided by the men, we developed our own additional references wherever possible. As one might expect, it is infrequent that critical references are volunteered. The additional references might come from any number of sources, including the superiors, peers, and subordinates from prior business relationships of the men. What we learned was that the CEO was considered bright, hard working, honest, experienced, and excellent in the marketing area, a good leader, strongly motivated to succeed, a little headstrong with a large ego, decisive and able to make tough decisions, weak in manufacturing and engineering, and, overall, very highly regarded. His weaknesses included a tendency to be overly optimistic and excessively loyal to his people, which he manifested by being too slow to make necessary personnel changes. The number-two man was also highly regarded and was somewhat similar in strengths. The technical members of the team seemed to be quite competent, but, due to the nature of their employment history references, we were not able to obtain answers to questions we had about them. We decided to investigate further in this area.

During the reference checking effort, we continued to make our own personal appraisal of the people through additional face-to-face business meetings as well as through a few social dinner visits.

We think it is very important to get to know people through several meetings and in different kinds of circumstances. A much better working relationship, both before and after a financing, can be developed if good communication, understanding, and rapport can be established. The determination of the degree to which people "wear well" is important to both parties.

Our overall impression of the management people at this point was very positive. The one element that was bothersome was evidence of a tendency toward stubbornness, coupled with procrastination in the personnel area. We considered this a potential major negative because, as the deal had been presented to us, management would own slightly over 50% of the company and, therefore, would be able to ignore counsel if they chose.

PRODUCT DEVELOPMENT

The incomplete development of the product was, of course, a concern to us, particularly because one functional element had not yet been proven. Management claimed this function was not very important and, in any case, easy to complete. Our marketing analysis convinced us that the function was important.

That raised two questions for us: (1) Was management not well informed about its own market, or were they not leveling with us? (2) What were the technical risks that would be assumed by going ahead with the financing before development was completed?

To answer the first question, we decided to do further market research by talking to additional people in the field, including potential users of the product and industry experts. We also re-contacted some of the previous references, with more concentration on this particular question. What we found was a bigger area of gray. To some potential users the feature in question was not critical; to others it was so important that they wouldn't purchase without it. And, of course, there were attitudes between these two extremes. This indicated that if the technical problems could not be overcome, the company wouldn't necessarily be out of business, but the total market size would be substantially reduced. The implication was that the valuation of the company (the price) would have to be lower to compensate for the possibility of a much smaller upside investment potential.

Additional discussions with management concerning the importance of the product feature convinced us that the difference in views we held from those we thought they held was honest and explainable and not the result of misrepresentations, which would have killed the deal immediately from our standpoint. There was, however, still a meaningful difference of opinion as to the impact on the company if this functional element could not be incorporated into the product.

To help us answer the question about the technical risk and to evaluate the competence of the two technical people we hired a consultant. We used a man who was employed in another company in which we had an investment. Because of our past experience with him, we had a high degree of confidence in his abilities and judgment and felt that his competence was high in the areas we were asking him to appraise. His reports indicated that he believed the feature could be developed, but he was concerned about the amount of development time and dollars required. There was, of course, no assurance of success.

MARKET ANALYSIS

Our analysis of the market included talking to industry experts, reading industry surveys and literature of the competing companies, and detailed questioning of the management. In obtaining an industry expert, you would like to find the universally best informed person who has had direct experience with the particular subject and is in fact an *expert*. Oftentimes, such a person does not exist or is a competitor. However, usually a number of persons can be identified who have sufficient experience to be of meaningful help. In this case, we were partially lucky. We could not find anyone who was broadly enough based to cover all aspects of the market that was being addressed by the company because its product cut across several market segments. Therefore, we tried to separate the problem. The company suggested one person, and we found a second one by following leads through several levels of subsequent references. With the two men we were able to develop most of the information we felt was appropriate in making a decision.

From all of the above, we became convinced that the product was a very real advance and that the market was large and ready to accept the product providing the company used a reasonable marketing effort.

The size of the market usually is a very important factor. We felt that in five years the annual shipments of products to the market in which this company would be competing could reach $200 million. Assuming that the technical feature in question was made part of the company's product offering, we believed that the company could attain about a 10% share of the market, or $20,000,000. Without the technical feature, however, the market size might be cut in half. This judgment ("guess" is probably a more accurate word) suggested that the risk of the functional technical feature's not working changed the potential of the operation from a high profit margin $20 million revenue business to a medium profit margin $10 million business, with an even greater impact on potential value. Instead of earning an expected $1,600,000 (8% net after tax on $20 million in sales) and being worth, say, $19,200,000 (a price/earnings ratio of 8). This was more than a fourfold reduction in potential value. Obviously, there are other factors involved in a return on investment evaluation, such as the amount of additional capital and, therefore, dilution that must be obtained as growth continues. The figures given only illustrate the effects of potential market size and market share on company value.

In appraising the market share that might be achieved, competition needed to be considered. There was no existing competitor who would be offering a comparable product. However, it was expected that, as a sizable market developed, competition would appear. Existing manufacturers of the products for this market could be expected to react with new features, new products, price reductions, or all of these. In addition, once the new product becomes visible and begins to make a market impact, new competitors will become interested in the market. These will include other startup companies and product introductions by companies in an associated field who recognize the market potential. In this case, the market appeared to be big enough to accommodate active, forceful competition.

The recognizable potential competitors were studied, their relative strengths appraised, and estimates made as to possible new company efforts. This, coupled with our market analysis, led to our guess that this company could reasonably capture 10% of the market.

CAPITAL ADEQUACY

After sizing up the market and the company's potential, the question of capital adequacy was considered. Doing this is of major importance, because if not enough money is raised, the investor is faced with several negative situations. First, more money will have to be raised, which will dilute the investor's ownership and lower the rate of return on which the investment decision was based. Second, if the company cannot raise the money, the investor is faced with the prospect of having to put up more money, if he is legally or financially able to do so, or lose a significant part of the original investment even though the company may be making good progress. Times change, and even though the company is progressing, outside money may not be available. Third, the company management will have to devote a substantial amount of time to the money-raising effort and, therefore, will be forced to reduce its attention to the problem of running the business. This is a high and very real cost to a young company, and sometimes it can be near fatal.

All of the above elements need to be balanced against trying to raise too much money. The greater the amount of money, the greater the number of partners needed in the deal, the more time it will take, and the greater the dilution to management and to the investor. The answer to "what is the right amount of money" depends on a number of factors. These include the investors' cash resources and willingness to provide future financing, the length of operating time that seems reasonable under the circumstances before reentering the "money-raising mode," and the probability that the indicated time will have enabled the company to make sufficient progress so that it can obtain additional funds at a higher price to reduce dilution.

In the case in question management's projections seemed unrealistic in several ways: sales growth rate and profit margins both seemed too high, and the debt position also seemed too large, relative to equity. A slower sales buildup would decrease the expected need for cash due to a lower requirement for working capital, but in this case lower profits would more than offset this benefit. The net result was a belief that at least another $1 million would be needed in 12 to 18 months, and probably a third financing would be required in the third or fourth year.

We then did an analysis of the company's prospective viability. We put emphasis on the salability of its products and the cost and capital structure of the business. In the product area, we took a user's point of view in looking at the benefits and costs of buying the company's product. We applied both the payback and present value methods of analysis. We looked at the various elements of user savings: reduced labor, high productivity, reduced material costs, less downtime, and some intangibles like safety and easier governmental compliance. We then compared the savings that would be made over a period of time with the initial costs plus extra marginal operating costs. It appeared to us that in a typical user environment the product would achieve payback within two years and an internal rate of return of approximately 40% per year, which in this industry was considered highly attractive. Based on this analysis and on our discussions with prospective customers, we concluded that customers would be willing to pay the proposed or even a higher sales price.

We then concentrated on the company's cost and capital structure. The cost of goods sold, operating expense levels, planned personnel levels, development expense levels, and the like were carefully evaluated for reasonableness. We concluded that, while the company's projections were too optimistic, there was sufficient margin in the product to sustain a profitable business. The overall business plan was well formulated in most areas, including manpower loading, new product development, marketing strategy, and overall business strategy.

We summed up our view of the proposal's pluses and minuses, made our own forecasts of the company's sales, earnings, and capital requirements, and did an analysis of the expected return on our investment at the proposed financing terms. We concluded that the return was not high enough for the risks we perceived. We weren't willing, therefore, to invest on the basis suggested by management, although we were sufficiently interested to want the investment on modified terms.

MAKING THE DEAL

After much discussion with the company on the terms of the deal, which, in addition to price, included type of security, seniority, and income, we and the company were able to narrow the gap substantially. The only major problem was the more optimistic view of the future held by management, as is generally the case. We were only able to break the deadlock by reluctantly agreeing to a "performance deal." This was accomplished by investing at a price that was acceptable to management but considered by us too high with a stipulation that the price would be subject to downward adjustment if the company did not meet its projections.

Successful levels of profit achievement or lack thereof were stipulated at which the price of our investment would be reduced, thereby increasing our ownership of the company. If management performed anywhere near its potential levels, they would receive their asking price, and we would be quite happy with that kind of performance. If they didn't perform, the price we paid would be reduced and the percentage of the company we owned would be increased, thereby bringing the valuation more in line with the "real value" as perceived by us. This also reduced our concern about the shortcomings of management, since our influence increased as results became less positive.

We dislike this kind of arrangement, however, and use it very infrequently because it can create a conflict or differences in motivations on certain issues and can get in the way of the most objective business decisions. For example, increasing research expenditures might be a wise long-run decision, but it decreases near-term earnings, thereby reducing the investment price and therefore diluting management's equity.

In this case we had high regard for the people involved, felt their objectives and ours were quite compatible, and were able to agree on how potential conflict situations would be handled in the future. We made the investment on that basis.

As mentioned, each investment is different and subject to varying degrees of objectivity, ranging from precise statistical analysis to almost total, seat-of-the-pants guessing. However, in the last several years, investment decisions within the venture community have increasingly involved very careful objective analysis and less reliance on instinctive reactions and guesswork.

The Key to Successful Leveraged Buyouts: Analysis of Management

GREGORY P. BARBER

There are many quantitative and qualitative aspects to the analysis undertaken by an outside equity investor considering a leveraged buyout proposal. It is difficult to segregate any of these aspects and place it uppermost on the list of ingredients that make a leveraged buyout successful. Clearly, the financial profile of the investment must be right. The product or service must have market acceptance, the financing must be appropriate, and the people must be capable of managing the company. Far too often the outside equity investor becomes enamored with quantitative items, such as profit margins, market share, historical growth rates, and so on, and becomes strictly qualitative about the people who will be responsible for producing the results necessary for a successful venture. We have tried to augment our own judgment (often called "gut feeling") with a quantitative review of the management we propose to support in an investment. We have also learned that risk increases proportionately with the learning curve that management must overcome. We have divided the risk spectrum into three sections which are described below.

1. We have found that the safest leveraged buyout is one that contemplates no management changes whatsoever. A good example of this is a corporate divestiture to the management group that has (and has had for some time) the operating responsibility for the business being divested. Not only is there a zero learning curve, but also the management will have full knowledge of potential problems that are not readily apparent to outsiders seeking to purchase the business.

    We always undertake a thorough investigation to uncover hidden liabilities, but nonetheless, we get great comfort from knowing that the individuals who have been running the business are willing to invest their own hard-earned money in the same venture.

    This type of situation is less traumatic for customers and vendors of the company, as they will continue to deal with the same people. Our investment in Company #1, which is described later in this article, exemplifies this type of management risk.

2. If an attractive opportunity presents itself and it does not include existing management, the risk is enhanced. This is obvious, as there is no longer an "insider" for the outside equity investor to participate with in the acquisition evaluation, and hidden liabilities could later surface. To hedge against this risk, the new investor can ask for more representations and warranties in the purchase agreement. These are valuable only if the seller is financially capable of satisfying future claims or a sufficient escrow is arranged. Nonetheless, an operating risk has been created, for the new management must take control and overcome a learning process.

    When this type of opportunity arises, we feel most comfortable if the new management has a successful track record in precisely the same business. This normally means that the new management has been with a direct competitor of the company being acquired. This competitive experience proves helpful in assessing acquisition risks in addition to shortening the learning curve.

    On the plus side, new management might very well bring a new perspective and vitality to the company. This type of situation represents greater risk and greater reward than the

"status quo" example described earlier. Our investment in Company #2 typifies this kind of situation.
3. When an outside equity investor ventures beyond the management parameters described in Examples 1 and 2, the risk factor will increase dramatically. At Narragansett Capital Corporation (NCC) we are fully aware that the leveraged financial approach we employ creates sufficient risk without being compounded by the uncertainty of whether management can be successful in the business under consideration. To underscore this concern, I have described our investment in Company #3. We did much soul-searching as to management's ability to make a transition from an industrial products to a consumer products business before agreeing to provide the necessary financing. This investment is off to a healthy start, and it is used to exemplify the outer limit of the management risk spectrum that we will entertain.

COMPANY #1

The financial profile of this investment created immediate interest on our part. As part of an overall corporate strategy to concentrate on branded consumer products, the parent company decided to divest this division, which operates as a converter of fabric for the home furnishings and home decorative industries. The price was set at a slight premium over book value and was fair as a multiple of historic and projected earnings. This financial profile suggested that our highly leveraged approach could be utilized, and the following financing package was arranged:

Senior Bank Revolving Credit	$4,250,000
NCC 10-Year Subordinated Loan	2,450,000
Equity	500,000
Total	$7,200,000

The earnings and cash flow of the business showed that the acquisition debt could be serviced properly, and our investigation revealed that the industry outlook was satisfactory. As for management, our investigation revealed the following.

The president and CEO had full profit and loss responsibility for this business for over 10 years. Furthermore, he had been a stockholder of the company when it was originally sold to the parent company in the early 1970s and had spent over 30 years with the company. The record showed that he was a consistent and proven money-maker in this industry, and his knowledge of the company was unquestionable. Clearly, he was a "10" on a scale of 10.

As for the second-tier operating managers, all of whom became our shareholder partners, their depth of experience was equally impressive. Among three individuals, there were nearly 90 years of experience in the industry of which 60 had been spent at this particular company. This combined in depth knowledge of the industry and the company proved to be very helpful in negotiating a satisfactory agreement with the seller.

We expect the business to be run exactly as it had been in the past. The continuation of their fine record will result in an excellent return on investment for all shareholders. These management characteristics, coupled with a sound financial profile, make for a very sound and safe investment from an outside equity investor's point of view.

COMPANY #2

This company operates 24 discount health and beauty aid stores in the greater Pittsburgh area. The two owner/managers decided to sell, and we were approached by an outside group seeking to purchase the company. This did not look like an attractive opportunity on the surface because of a relatively flat sales and earnings performance in recent years. Our interest in the investment changed dramatically after meeting the proposed new management team. The key operating manager had excellent credentials in the health and beauty aid business. His 17 years of experience began at the level of assistant store manager and progressed through his present position as a district manager with profit and loss responsibility for 60 stores. His two proposed partners augmented this "hands-on" operating experience with strong administrative and control skills developed in running their own successful wholesale drug business.

During the initial meetings, it became obvious that our proposed partners had identified the strengths and weaknesses of the business. This, in itself, was not particularly significant, but their detailed plan to exploit strengths and correct weaknesses led us to believe that they had an excellent chance of improving the present performance. The new CEO proposed to revamp all key areas, including purchasing, merchandising, staffing, and so on, while the other partners would concentrate on the implementation of new inventory controls and management information systems. The demonstrated track record of all the individuals in the areas in which they would contribute convinced us to make this investment.

It should be noted that the financial profile of this investment was fairly conservative. In other words, the price was a relatively low multiple of earnings, and the new company would be able to meet its debt obligations even if earnings decreased. The debt service coverage ratio was initially over two to one, and it would increase to three or four to one once projections were met. It would be ill-advised to introduce new management into an investment that financially offers little or no margin for error. We consider this type of investment to have more opportunities for a higher return on investment than Example #1 because new management will implement new ideas and bring needed vitality to a rather stagnant company. Nonetheless, we will only attempt this if our downside position is limited by a conservative financial structure.

COMPANY #3

This 100-year-old company became available in mid-1979 when the major shareholder chose to devote more time to personal activities. It was brought to our attention by an individual who had been seeking to purchase a company for the past several months. The business itself had an excellent record as a manufacturer of hair care products, and the proposed price was fair relative to earnings and assets being acquired. Our leveraged formula appeared to be appropriate, and the following financing was arranged:

Senior Bank Term Loan	$ 900,000
NCC 10-Year Subordinated Loan	900,000
Equity	200,000
Total	$2,000,000

The proposal looked acceptable financially, and the business had a stable earnings record. The management analysis was considerably more difficult. First, there were to be no members of existing management included as stockholders. In addition, the present top management planned to leave the company almost immediately after the sale. There would be no employment or consulting contracts with these individuals. Second, the new team (our partners) were coming from outside of the industry. The company operated as a consumer products business selling to the major chains and mass merchandisers. Our partners had backgrounds in the plastics industry, but of a commercial rather than consumer nature. Nonetheless, after considerable deliberation, we decided to proceed.

What factors induced us to take this risk?

1. It was a very conservative capitalization in which historical earnings would enable the new company to pay interest and principal on its debt and have a substantial surplus. This conservative capitalization would enable the business to withstand a few errors in judgment made by the new management.
2. The capabilities of the new management were verified by a number of good references who emphasized the strong integrity of the individuals. The latter is important in any evaluation of management, but especially so in this case. We felt that it was absolutely necessary for management to communicate freely and honestly with us as they underwent the learning process in their new business. They have, in fact, encountered problems that were not fully exposed prior to closing. We have been kept fully informed, however, and many of these problems are now behind us. The investment seems to be headed in the right direction. We feel strongly at NCC that good news can wait, but bad news cannot.

In summary, management analysis can be a very difficult process. We feel that while "gut feeling" and the "right chemistry" are important factors, the outside equity investor should have hard data to support convictions about management. Our business is one of selecting winners, and we must always use all available resources to make decisions.

WHEN AND HOW TO GO PUBLIC

The public marketplace is an uncertain friend for the small, growing company. In the 1960s virtually any company could raise money by "going public." This environment shifted radically in the 1970s, and by 1975 public financing was almost impossible for the small company. In the last three years the public marketplace has become more receptive to new issues, and companies which can demonstrate growth potential have an excellent opportunity to achieve a successful public offering.

The decision to go public can be both tantalizing and traumatic. Although it may extend unfettered capital to a growing firm, it also exposes the embryonic business to a level of public scrutiny that may be more problematic than the watchful eyes of private investors. The public market is unforgiving in its business evaluation and slow to regain its confidence. A company experiencing its early growing pains may not be able to withstand public examination and pressure, and therefore it is imperative that management carefully examine the advantages and disadvantages of "going public" before succumbing to the lure of the public market. The venture capitalists' tactic of waiting for their portfolio companies to display the strengths of a viable independent business, before they recommend a public offering, should also be kept in mind by prospective entrepreneurs.

The following articles discuss "going public" as a viable alternative for the small company in need of growth capital and highlight the pitfalls awaiting the newly public company. In addition to presenting guidelines for dealing with investment bankers both before and after the public offering, these articles also offer useful advice for the public company assuming the new role of dealing with stockholders and stock analysts.

It should be recognized that a newly public company will not normally be abandoned by its venture capital investors, because these investors rarely sell their ownership positions in a public offering. They continue to offer guidance and, in fact, achieve their greatest financial gains after a portfolio company attains success in the public marketplace.

Public Financing for Smaller Companies

PETER W. WALLACE

Since the end of 1977 we have seen an increased strengthening of demand in the marketplace for the offerings of smaller companies going public for the first time. Public financing has become a viable alternative for the well-managed smaller company exhibiting an above average growth rate and having the prospect for continued growth over the years ahead.

Hambrecht & Quist has specialized in raising money for the emerging high growth rate companies, generally in technology-related businesses. Since the inception of our firm in 1969 we have managed or co-managed more than 60 public offerings for a total of approximately $500 million. More than a third of these offerings, and over half the dollar total, have occurred since mid-1978. Looking back at the new issue market, in 1969 there were over 1,000 new offerings, which raised an estimated $2.6 billion for the issuing companies. The pace declined steadily in the next few years until in 1975 there were six initial offerings, which raised a total of $34 million, and the level remained low for the next couple of years, with a steady increase year to year starting in 1978. Despite the anticipation and eventual realization of a recession in

1980, the public market has remained strong for the better quality smaller companies, where investors are looking for growth opportunities that will create equity gains at a rate substantially above that of inflation. It is important to recognize that the availability of the public market at any given point in time is highly dependent upon a variety of conditions, including the general state of the economy, inflationary trends, interest rates, and so on. In this article, we will presume the existence of a viable public market (as is presently the case) and will deal with the factors to be considered by corporate management in assessing the merits of public financing as one of several alternatives. We will consider the principal criteria of the marketplace, the advantages and disadvantages of a public offering from the point of view of the issuing company, the process of selection of an underwriter and a description of the typical sequence of events that occur in the process of "going public" once the decision has been made.

CRITERIA OF THE MARKETPLACE

From the "hot markets" and "concept companies" of the late 1960s we have seen a development in the sophistication of the criteria by which the marketplace evaluates young growing companies with respect to their stock issues. We have also seen the emergence of the institutional buyers (banks, pension funds, money managers, investment advisers) as the leading factor in the new issue market, in contrast to the previous dependence of that market upon the individual or "retail" buyer. The result has been a more analytical approach, a higher degree of selectivity, and a more consistent set of long-term objectives.

The primary goal, of course, is the achievement of a steadily increasing equity value through growth in sales and earnings. In these days of high inflation rates and high interest rates, a company must exhibit an above average growth potential in order to interest the investor, who sees alternative uses for his capital in low-risk, high-yield debt investments, and who needs to achieve "something extra" to compensate him for the risk of tying up his capital in a small, unseasoned company. In the past year or so, the companies that have been coming to market with initial public offerings have generally been capable of consistent annual growth rates in the range of 30% to 50%, and in some cases have exceeded 100% with the prospect for continuation of that rate for at least a year or two more. In general, these companies have achieved an annual revenue rate that typically is at least in the $15-$20 million range and in some cases has been a great deal higher. Again, speaking in generalities, net income is usually above an annual rate of $1 million.

While there are many exceptions to the foregoing criteria (particularly in the smaller issues, often sold on a "best efforts" basis rather than in a firm underwriting), the ability to sustain after-market interest in the stock of a newly public company is significantly diminished when a company has not achieved the size, profitability, and growth outlined above.

UNDERWRITERS' CRITERIA

For an investment banker to manage a successful offering, he must be sensitive to the requirements of the marketplace that he is serving. Accordingly, when an underwriter is approaching a potential corporate client he will be keeping in mind the market criteria described, while at the same time recognizing additional fundamental criteria that must be met in order for him to offer the stock with confidence, make a trading market in the securities, and continue to recommend purchases by his clients in the after-market.

Clearly the underwriter must be enthusiastic about the basic business in which the corporate client is engaged. For instance, if a company has had a superb growth record but its industry will be negatively affected by technology changes, increased major competition, recession-induced problems, or by other factors that will change the fundamental outlook, the underwriter will then think carefully about the wisdom of managing a stock offering for the company in question. An overriding consideration, in any event, is the quality of the people who are running the company. An investment banker must assess the capability, integrity, intelligence, "toughness," and desire to achieve, as well as the general objectives of the management group as a key part of his decision to proceed with an offering.

The quality of the financial record is also of major importance. The Securities and Exchange Commission (SEC) requires a summary of operation for the past five years and audited income statements for the past three years (with exceptions for companies whose existence has been of a shorter duration).

PUBLIC OFFERING FROM THE ISSUER'S VIEWPOINT

The question of whether or not to go public is not trivial. Once a company has taken the step to offer shares of its stock to the public marketplace, it becomes subject to a degree of regulatory and market scrutiny from which it was previously insulated. This in turn will create additional demands upon management time and will inevitably play a part in operating decisions.

Let's take a look at the basic advantages and disadvantages of a public offering. On the plus side would be the following:

1. If a company is acceptable to the public market, its securities will generally command a higher price than in a private equity placement. This means that equity capital can be raised with minimal dilution.
2. Once a company's securities have become seasoned in the public market, the mechanism is in place for further public financings to bring in additional equity capital as needed to support a continuing growth program.
3. A viable public market creates liquidity, which can be important for shareholders in general and particularly for founders and managers who may have substantial holdings in the company's stock.
4. The public marketplace provides an objective and credible measure of the value of the company's stock, which is of importance in attracting new management talent through equity participation, in motivating employee shareholders, and in providing for acquisitions a medium of exchange with a readily acceptable valuation.
5. Being publicly held can increase a company's stature or image to its customers, suppliers, bankers, and others.

On the negative side of the ledger would be the following:

1. Going public requires a detailed disclosure of the company's affairs in its offering prospectus. This reveals to competitors, customers, employees, and the public at large many details of the company's business that it may feel more comfortable keeping to itself.
2. A public company is subjected to reporting requirements by the SEC that will mean, in general, the preparation of a public document on a quarterly basis. In addition, the requirements of the stock market and the public investors for continuing information about the company's affairs will mean the initiation of a formal management program to furnish periodic reports and maintain communication with analysts, portfolio managers, major shareholders, and a variety of others.
3. The expectations of a public shareholder group will put considerable emphasis on maintenance of a smooth pattern of operations and growth. Deviations from an established growth trend line that can be accommodated readily within a private company in order to focus on a particular development effort, a special marketing program, or other unusual expenditure are much more difficult to communicate to the public in a way that will avoid resultant fluctuations in the price of the stock.
4. Finally, the costs of the offering itself are not insignificant. In addition to the underwriter's compensation, or "spread," there are expenses of attorneys, auditors, financial printers, and a number of additional costs all of which can add up to $150,000–$200,000 even for a small offering. These costs obviously have to be weighed against the benefits of a public offering as compared with other methods of financing.

SELECTION OF AN INVESTMENT BANKER

The investment banker who is chosen to be the company's managing underwriter performs a variety of roles. Immediately in connection with the public offering he will organize a syndicate of other investment bankers to achieve appropriate distribution of the company's stock, both on a geographical basis and to provide a balance between institutional and individual stockholders. Once the stock has been issued to the public, the managing underwriter assumes responsibility for a continued sponsorship of the corporate client to the financial community. This includes making a market in the company's stock, providing analytical reports by the securities research department, organizing presentations to groups of investors and potential investors, and generally assisting the corporation in establishing a strong following within the financial community. Among the characteristics that a company should look for in selecting an investment banker are the following:

Reputation

The stature and professional reputation of the investment banker within the financial community. This will affect the ability to form a strong syndicate of firms, and it will influence the quality of investors who can be attracted to the offering.

Experience

The investment banker's experience in underwriting issues of companies in the same or similar industries. This will be important in the degree of credibility accorded the underwriter's presence by the investment community. It will also influence his ability to price the issue accurately.

Research Capability

Because the managing underwriter will be looked to by the financing community as a primary source of information about the newly public company, it is important that the selected investment banking firm have experienced analysts closely following the industry in which the company does its business. The reputation of an individual analyst on "the street" can have a strong effect on the degree of interest that can be sustained in the company's stock.

Market-Making Capability

When a company first issues stock to the public, the shares will be traded on the "over-the-counter" market. A number of investment banking firms will become the market makers in this new stock. The role of the managing underwriter is generally to provide leadership in the market-making function and to provide sufficient depth on both the buy and sell side of the market so that it will insure liquidity for even large shareholders. This requires the investment banking firm to devote sufficient capital to the market making activity so that meaningful long or short positions can be maintained in the day-to-day market-making activities.

Distribution Capability

Different investment banking firms have different client bases, some emphasizing institutional accounts, others primarily dealing with individuals, still others having an international emphasis as opposed to domestic, and so forth. A company should determine whether the investment banker can, in fact, distribute the company's stock effectively to a client base that can serve as a strong element of ongoing market interest in the stock.

In general, a company manager seeking an investment banker should take the time to be sure he is comfortable not only with the people with whom he will be directly involved initially, but also with those who will have ongoing responsibility for market making, research, sales sponsorship, and so forth. He should talk with the managements of other corporate clients of the proposed investment banker and find out first hand what their experience has been and how they feel about a long-term relationship with the particular underwriter. The process of selection of an investment banker is that of selecting a particular kind of professional who can provide a variety of services over a long period of time.

TYPICAL SEQUENCE OF EVENTS

While each individual case has its own characteristics and its own time schedule, a typical pattern might be as follows: The XYZ Company has reached a point in its growth where it recognizes the need for additional capital to finance growth in the year or two ahead. The company may have been in business for a number of years and private investors who provided the initial capital are interested in seeing some degree of liquidity and a measure of value on their shares. In a series of meetings, the XYZ directors determine that it is appropriate for the company to seek a public offering. The management is directed to discuss this possibility with a number of underwriters and to ask those who appear to be both suitable and interested to make formal presentations to the board of directors. The proposed underwriters will each make visits to the company to become acquainted with management and operations prior to submitting their proposals. Finally a selection is made by the board and management of the company and the formal process commences.

When the preparation of the underwriting is to begin, an "all hands" meeting is held involving the company management, the managing underwriter, company counsel, underwriter's counsel, and auditors. At this time, a time schedule is laid out for the demanding task of preparing the registration statement to be filed with the SEC as well as the subsequent events that will involve the marketing of the proposed issue. A part of the registration statement is the prospectus, which will be distributed publicly, and which describes the company's history and operations in some detail. The preparation of the registration materials will typically take 30 to 60 days, a time period that may be extended, if necessary, to accommodate the completion of an audit.

Once the registration statement is filed with the SEC, the preliminary prospectuses are printed and the marketing process commences. At this time, the underwriter will invite other investment banking firms into the underwriting syndicate, and the final syndicate may be composed of 50 to 70 firms. As these firms accept positions in the syndicate their salesmen begin to talk with clients and furnish them with prospectuses. Meanwhile, the managing underwriter will typically organize a series of presentations by company management in various key cities where significant institutional or individual investor interest can be found. Perhaps a half dozen to a dozen cities will be visited over a period of one to two weeks.

At the same time the SEC processes the registration and ultimately responds (usually within three to four weeks) with a series of comments, questions, or requests for additional information. The prospectus is then modified as needed to conform with the

SEC request, and when the SEC is satisfied with the content, it will permit the issue to become effective.

Immediately prior to the offering becoming effective, the underwriter and the company have the last of a series of price discussions and set the price of the offering, which will then be incorporated into an amended prospectus. The revised prospectus with the price amendment then becomes a final prospectus that is printed and distributed after the offering has become effective. As soon as the offering is effective, sales can be confirmed by the members of the syndicate to their clients. Prior to effectiveness, they can do nothing more than take indications of interest.

The final step will be the closing, generally five business days after the offering becomes effective. At this time, the money changes hands and the offering is completed.

CONCLUSION

The public marketplace should be considered as one of several valid alternatives for the small growing company. There are, however, both advantages and disadvantages to a public offering and these should be weighed carefully before attempting to go forward. The proper selection of the investment banker who will be managing underwriter for the issue is of key importance not only to the success of the issue, but perhaps even more important, to the maintenance of long-term interest in the stock once it becomes publicly held. Finally, market timing is important because the availability of the public market to smaller companies can change, from time to time, with changes in the economy and with changes in investor attitudes toward the stock market.

Financial Public Relations— A Key Ingredient After Going Public

EDWARD G. NOVOTNY

WHY YOU NEED A PR PROGRAM

Successful public offerings do not just happen. They are the result of hard work, both in planning and marketing by the underwriters. To sell a new issue, underwriters will create considerable public interest in your company's stock.

Let's assume that your underwriters have done an excellent job. They have managed to sell your company's stock at a multiple of 10 times projected earnings and your company is growing at the rate of 20% a year.

But once you have left the cocoon of the underwriters, you emerge into the cold world where more than 20,000 corporations are competing for the attention of the investment community. A relatively small percentage of these companies are treated to a price-earnings multiple of more than five, six, or seven times earnings.

Part of your corporate strategy in going public in the first place is to maintain an attractive price-earnings multiple for your stock, perhaps as much as 12 times earnings, so that it will be easier to sustain future growth rates by additional equity offerings. The purposes of this are to enable you to acquire certain companies that fit into your corporate plans without diluting your present earnings and to improve the status of your company as it competes for new customers and maintains relationships with suppliers. These objectives will not be met—or at least not met anywhere as effectively as anticipated—if your stock drops to the average price-earnings ratio of an average OTC company. The question then is how do you continue to sustain sufficient interest of the financial community in your company so that the price-earnings multiple for your shares will remain at, or increase beyond, present levels.

Certainly the major ingredient is your company's ability to continue to perform as expected by the financial community. A second—and perhaps almost as important—is a continuous awareness by the financial community of the performance and quality of your company. This is the role of financial public relations. Financial public relations is the technique by which you can communicate effectively to the investment community—analysts, institutions, individual investors, and others—that your company is worthy of special consideration beyond that of the average publicly owned company. This article will discuss various alternatives by which you can develop your own public relations program, the objectives that you might build into such a program, and how you can utilize outside counsel to perform these services.

HELL . . . OR SHANGRI-LA

Going public can be like entering an entirely new world. Where once no one seemed to know or care about your privately owned company, now shareholders, the press, the SEC, and a host of pressure groups appear relentlessly intent upon knowing *everything*. Just as for public officeholders, probing eyes and ears are everywhere. It is enough to spark paranoia. For the unprepared this can be hell, but for the businessman who has drawn up a thoughtful plan, it can be a rewarding experience.

A typical financial public relations plan for a company that has just had its initial public offering may include:

Publications
- Annual report
- Quarterly reports
- Corporate fact book
- Key management presentations

Editorial Activities
- Financial news releases
- Editorial monitoring and interviews
- Business and financial articles

Financial Community Relations
- Preparation of typical questions that management can expect an analyst to ask by telephone and at meetings with the financial community. Of course, answers to such questions must be prepared.
- Development of interest in the company by arranging analysts' visits
- Group breakfast, luncheon, or after-market meetings
- Reports on current market opinion
- Daily contact with analysts, portfolio managers, brokers

Stockholders' Communications
- Annual meeting presentations
- Reports on hightlights of annual meetings
- Periodic contact with large institutional holders

Stock Movements
- Periodic contact with market maker or floor specialist
- Analysis of stock transfer sheets, major shifts in holdings, geographic sales

Coordination of Communications Program
- Coordination of financial public relations program with corporate public relations, advertising, and sales promotion plans

Timetable and Budget
- Breakdown of proposed time schedule
- Realistic estimates of total costs of each project

IS IT A BIRD . . . IS IT A PLANE . . .

The majority of PR people come from vastly diverse backgrounds. Some never finished college, others hold a graduate degree in English literature, finance, journalism, communications, law, or engineering. Many got their start as news or report writers, while others began in marketing, sales, and advertising. They range in age from 18 to over 70, and more talented women are entering the field today than ever before. Just as corporate executives do, PR practitioners come in all shapes and sizes. Some are specialists—financial and investor relations, trade publicity, press contact, international communications writing—while others are generalists who combine a broad range of corporate and financial public relations skills.

Few PR people work from nine to five—let alone a five-day week. Like unforeseen management problems, public relations problems seem to develop at the most inconvenient times of the day—in the early morning and late at night. There is a unique predilection for PR problems to develop on weekends. Just as any other professionals, PR counselors become wiser with experience, but as in sports, there can sometimes be a trade-off between age and cost. From a cost viewpoint, a young PR professional can be easy on the corporate pocketbook, especially if management's counseling needs are neither critical nor immediate. While the younger PR professionals have not run the obstacle course hundreds of times, there is an opportunity with them to bring someone in at the ground level and let them grow with the business. The deciding factor for any business relationship, of course, is that the person employed should be chosen with the same care as a marriage partner. In fact, in a publicly held company PR counsel and top management will probably spend more hours together trying to resolve corporate problems than they will at home with their mates.

IN-HOUSE, AGENCY, OR BOTH?

No two companies share exactly the same type of public relations structure, let alone pay the same amount of staff salaries or fees to PR agencies. It's obvious that no two companies in today's diversified corporate world have exactly the same needs, nor do their PR functions evolve in the same way or over a similar period of time.

Most public relations departments have slowly evolved, both in size and importance—no huge staff has arrived on the scene overnight. In even the smallest company, someone usually acts in a public relations capacity. The chief executive officer communicates with and inspires employees; the treasurer gets the company's story across to the financial community; the sales manager gets an appealing message to potential customers. As a company grows, so do public relations duties—until a need for help is clearly identified, because of obvious conflicts with other corporate duties of management. As a company grows, the chairman, president, vice-president of finance, the sales manager, and the advertising director simply can't find enough hours in the day to handle PR projects. This is especially true when a company goes public.

Of course, there are other ways of developing a PR department, depending on the responsibilities involved, the number of company operations, their location, and size. If PR people are required to be on the job day and night, the initial move may be to hire a public relations director. The dollar cost for such a person, depending on experience, can be as low as a middle management salary. In some areas of the country the salary can be as low as $15,000 to $20,000. Some PR directors of major corporations earn well over $100,000. Many companies, on the other hand, prefer to choose a director from a large, experienced staff at a PR agency and, thereby, have the flexibility of adjusting expenditures to their business needs. All costs discussed are only very generalized ranges included for the sake of illustration and should not be applied to any particular PR project or program.

Some small publicly held companies with limited funds use PR agencies to help them produce annual reports, quarterly reports, and speeches for annual meetings. This certainly is not the most sophisticated program because public relations should be philosophically—yet practically—applied to all key areas of a company's business. Using a PR agency in this way, however, is cheap and can be paid for on either an hourly, daily, weekly, monthly, or project basis. A local free-lance writer, for example, may research a feature story for very few dollars, while an agency may take on the complicated task of producing an annual report for several thousand dollars. Depending on the number of professionals involved and whether they are junior writers or senior executives, agencies may charge as low as $25 to $50 an hour or over $100 an hour. The charge depends on location, costs involved, and the degree of executive talent required. While one agency may accept clients on a project basis, others will not accept a new account unless a full PR program is mandated and an agreement signed to cover work for a minimum period of a year. A public relations agency's price structure is determined by the same factors as is the largest manufacturer's—staff, landlords, and light bills must be paid.

Other companies begin with an in-house counsel, then supplement their PR program with agency counselors. An agency can be especially useful if a company needs the services of a very experienced staff or has many unforeseen PR needs—needs that may mean radical shifts in manpower requirements or simultaneous projects in several cities here or abroad.

Choosing in-house or agency counselors should be done with the same care as bringing aboard an attorney, an accountant, a new sales manager, an outside director, or an investment banker. Like anything else in this world, it takes effort, time, and a great deal of shopping. Credentials can be deceiving, but extensive personal interviews can be revealing, especially when supplemented by comments from former clients or employers, associates, and the press. In the process of checking an agency's qualifications, it is easy enough to check their reputations against each other and measure their ideas and approaches to the company's PR program needs.

The critical decision should be based on an evaluation of the extent to which the people involved will give their best efforts and devote the necessary time to learning the company's business—its nuances, hopes, and aspirations. It is also important to remember when weighing the merits of an agency that being large doesn't necessarily mean it is best. Public relations is a one-on-one business, and a small company can easily get lost in the vast stables of a giant public relations firm.

. . . COULD IT BE SUPERMAN?

On the job, the public relations executive needs direct access to top management and a commitment by the powers that be to back the PR strategies designed to achieve the specific corporate and financial objectives. This may sound logical and basic, but many competent PR in-house professionals spend their careers at major corporations frustrated by unenlightened management who have absolutely no idea of the potential of an effective public relations program. To add insult to injury, the necessary budgets to support PR projects are chopped to pieces so that mediocre results are absolutely guaranteed. Thanks to enlightened business writers and a growing stress on continuing education for corporate leaders, this situation is slowly changing, and public relations is becoming an integral element in modern corporate planning.

It is important to note, however, that public relations has its limitations. It can get a corporate story to the decision makers, but it can't change the bottom line on an earnings report; it can reach potential investors, but it can't kid anyone when the results are poor; it can expose management's talent and achievements, but it can't play Merlin the Magician when the chief executive officer is caught in an outright lie or falls flat on his face. Unlike Rumpelstiltskin, public relations counselors cannot weave gold out of straw. Alchemy just isn't part of a modern PR program. More important, public relations practitioners—like physicians, attorneys, and accountants before them—have worked hard to purge their ranks of those frauds who crept into their ranks by promising blue skies while leading companies into utter oblivion—or on the carpet before the SEC.

It is critical to financial public relations success that the PR man or woman be the most knowledgeable person available. The PR person must keep up to date on the latest pronouncements from the SEC, as well as on the current thinking among investor relations circles. The financial relations specialist must work closely with a company's legal staff to make sure that the letter of the law—and the spirit of the law—are followed closely. The SEC has made this clear in recent years by citing several financial public relations counselors who failed to recognize, in the SEC's eyes, that they shared the responsibility for management's alleged wrongdoings. Watergate and other cover-ups where PR advisors allegedly played key roles have also placed increased public pressure on the practitioner. Screen and TV writers have not helped the situation. They have told audiences for years that PR men and women are propagandists, hucksters, deceptive press agents, masters of obfuscation, and practitioners of the blackest arts. Nothing could be further from the truth, and it is naive to believe anyone can be fooled for long in today's tough investment environment.

ART VS. SCIENCE: GETTING IT DOWN ON PAPER

With management commitment and a professional PR counselor, the company is ready to get details of its PR plan on paper. The philosophy of a PR plan is no different from that of a corporate plan. It should be geared to corporate objectives and matched to PR strategies, then implemented by specific public relations activities, including both ongoing and special projects. Like a corporate plan, it should contain both short- and long-range plans and best estimates on proposed expenditures.

A PR plan should not be a complex and lengthy document, nor should the language employed be Middle Greek or early Swahili. Getting to the point quickly, concisely, and clearly is a guiding principle of good planning for PR people. As professional communicators, PR people can best reflect their talents in a corporate financial relations program memorandum by conciseness and clarity.

The two problems many PR people overlook in structuring a program are building into it flexibility and remembering that, like an important investment, it needs constant monitoring. Flexibility can be as simple as allowing enough time to do a project right, remembering that public relations is a business of unforeseen opportunities, challenges—and crises. Monitoring doesn't mean hovering over a typewriter or installing television cameras in the PR office, but making sure that periodic reports are reviewed with top management to insure that the program is on the right track, progressing as scheduled, and sure to achieve its goals as planned. Like sound financial controls, monitoring can sound a warning bell so that adjustments can be made before goals are missed and ulcers fester.

THE PROGRAM: CURRENT CONSIDERATIONS

No two corporate financial public relations programs are alike, but there are several elements that all sound programs have in common in contacts within and without the financial community.

Financial Communications

Once a company goes public, there are some basic reporting requirements that concern the PR counsel. These depend, of course, on whether the company lists on an exchange and on the attitude of its management toward shareholders. Some unenlightened companies do as little as possible, while others go out of their way to let everyone interested know the pertinent facts about the company's operations. It is clear from the spirit of the SEC—and pressure from the press and the public—that management, accountants, and PR counselors are under the gun to reveal more than ever about corporate operations. Moreover, recent recessions have created a wiser financial community, which ranks corporate credibility high on the investment criteria list. Aiding this trend are a wide range of corporate investigators—business reporters, crusading accountants, and attorneys—whose prime motivation is exposing corporate cover-ups. Today's corporate environment demands "telling it like it is" and maintaining credibility with current and potential investors. Thus financial public relations is concerned with communicating this information clearly and accurately through interim and annual reports, periodic news releases, letters to shareholders, quarterly newsletters, and press interviews.

Press Contact

One of the most important PR functions is working with the press to get the company's story across to opinion makers, the financial community, government officials, and current and prospective stockholders. Sometimes this may also mean *not* getting the company in the press when it could hurt the company unfairly. This activity, generally referred to as "defensive PR," is one of the most critical areas of public relations because it can sometimes mean the difference between a high multiple—and a penny stock. In most instances, the secret is getting to know *all* business writers who could write about the company and developing a reputation with them for straight talk and prompt replies to inquiries.

Management can play a key role in press activities. Success is as simple as taking the time to meet with important news writers and editors, making an effort to expose the company's executive talent, and always remembering that everyone respects managements that consistently exceed their conservative growth projections.

Counseling

If there is a critical element in a PR program, it is counseling and developing PR strategies to cope with unforeseen problems and opportunities. This means utilizing PR practitioners with experience and sound judgment. It may be as simple as an approach to a due diligence meeting or as complex as a master plan for analyst meetings in a dozen U.S. financial capitals. This counseling activity should not only be directed to a company's financial relations program, but also coordinated with all of the company's corporate communications programs so that a total promotional thrust is created.

Financial Community

Next to a company's commercial and investment bankers, analysts, advisory service people, writers, brokers, fund managers, and officers of institutions are very important. This is the nitty-gritty part of a PR practitioner's job, the part that some refer to as "the bloody-knuckle task." Mail and telephone are rarely as effective as going door to door to tell a company's story. Although publicly held companies try to touch base with the financial community, most fail to do it frequently enough. As a result, the overall effect is lost because the company message is not reinforced on a regular basis. For the novice, there are many reference books and computerized list services that can be helpful, but the most effective PR technique is that of simply getting out of the office and into the financial community meeting with decision makers in their own backyards. Managers who take vacations abroad should not overlook opportunities to meet with potential foreign investors in major capital markets. This can be done by picking up a telephone and asking the company's U.S. bank or friendly local broker for some names, then extending luncheon invitations to three or four of the best prospects.

Analysis

An important area that is commonly overlooked is "monitoring," or continually reviewing the financial PR program as it unfolds and adjusting it accordingly for maximum effectiveness. One very useful document for analysis is the stock transfer sheets, which can offer some idea of leading patterns, geographic interest, and the identity of substantial holders of the company's stock. The result of this planning should be a brief one-page analysis produced each month to pinpoint what key PR activities were undertaken in the 30-day period and what is planned for the coming month or two. These monthly reports can also be very helpful in reviewing PR plans and achievements with stockholders, banks, and brokers.

Insuring Effectiveness: The PR Audit

For more mature, larger publicly held companies—those that have had ongoing financial public relations programs for several years—there is a periodic need to evaluate the effectiveness of past and current programs. Obviously, to achieve an objective opinion, an outside consultant should be used, such as a public relations agency that is familiar with the type of PR program used by the company. The evaluation study is confidential and the cost of the audit is determined in advance of hiring the consultant. Costs are usually set on a project-only basis and are geared to the size of the company's operations and the extent to which the consultant is expected to research the PR activities. For example, while one company may simply wish to have its current program reviewed and critiqued for additional suggestions, another company may want to totally revamp its staff, structure an aggressive international plan, or develop a full-time speech bureau for its regional managers.

Whether done internally or with outside consultants, a PR audit can be an invaluable project to undertake on a periodic basis. It is a logical technique to insure that everything that can be done is being done. In the same way that auditors double-check the work of a corporate accounting staff, the PR audit provides an additional objective way to keep the corporate program on track.

Financial Public Relations: Tomorrow

No one has a crystal ball, but there are certain trends that are clear in the field of corporate and financial public relations. Like anyone in business today PR people must know more, read more, and work harder to perform key roles in the corporate makeup. Public relations practitioners are getting a more specialized education, developing more skills and techniques, and accepting, to a greater extent, the responsibility of weeding out those who do not meet the standards of the profession. Where once PR counselors received directives via interoffice mail, now many of them are recommending hard-hitting strategies and spelling out their ideas across the table at board of directors meetings. And, when appropriate, PR counsel speaks for the company, taking public responsibility for a company's plans, defending its actions, criticizing its adversaries, and getting the company's story across to the financial community.

Public relations can be a potent—and practical—financial marketing tool. Enlightened managers of companies that are going public should make it an integral part of the corporate plan.

Management's Responsibilities Change When a Company Becomes Publicly Held

BELMONT TOWBIN

The advantages and disadvantages of "going public" are adequately discussed in other sections of this book. These remarks are directed toward company managements that have already studied the problems of a public offering and have decided that the pluses outweight the minuses.

This discussion is not meant for the company that goes public to take advantage of a short-term trend, as many did during the early 1970s. Rather, it is directed to companies that could raise capital more advantageously through a public offering and that believe in the future. Such a company will be interested in a public market so that its success can be reflected in public enthusiasm for its shares so that its future progress can benefit the old owners, the broad management group, employees, and the new shareholders.

What new responsibilities are imposed on the management of this company now that it has "gone public"? First, the management must recognize that it now lives "in a goldfish bowl" and that there will be no secrets. There is the new type of board of directors, which might include someone designated by the underwriters plus others who are responsible to all stockholders and not just to management. Conclusions will have to be carefully thought out and justified by facts and figures rather than being intuitive, "seat of the pants" decisions.

Conflicts of interest between management and public stockholders become obvious. The company plane in Palm Beach in February is harder to explain when the business has several hundred partners (stockholders) than if ownership is concentrated in a few hands. Perquisites, such as expense accounts, country clubs, and travel must be more carefully scrutinized.

Reporting procedures to stock exchanges and the Securities and Exchange Commission and restrictions on purchase and sale of shares require vigilance unknown in the private company. Inclusion of the company lawyer on the board and/or his attendance at meetings is helpful.

The requirement of quarterly reporting demands more detailed short-range planning and, at times, decisions that adversely affect long-range programs. For example, an expenditure for research that will not show immediate results may have to be sacrificed so as not to damage the public image of "growth." This is not to say that sound business decisions are to be sacrificed for the sake of a superficial public image, but management must be aware that public companies are affected by special short-range problems and image-making decisions.

The management of a public company must accept the dissipation of some of its time to satisfy the inquiries of shareholders and security analysts. Such diversions can be handled to some extent by designating a junior officer to handle inquiries. The senior officers can limit most activity of this type to meetings two to four times a year with larger groups. The company is competing for investor attention with thousands of other public companies, and if this area is neglected, many of the benefits of public ownership will be lost.

As officers of a public company, management must recognize that proxy statements will show their salaries, stock holdings, retirement benefits, and yearly changes therein. This invasion of privacy can affect their decisions in union negotiations, in levels of executive compensation, and often in the conduct of their private lives. To repeat, in a public company every management decision must be considered as one that may be critically reviewed by many others. This is not necessarily a disadvantage, as it does tend to make decisions more deliberate and perhaps better thought out.

In a publicly held company, management must be committed to significant growth, on a year to year basis, or many of the reasons for going public will be negated. The market simply isn't interested in nice companies with a flat performance, and, therefore, management must be committed to fostering significant growth of the business as an integral management policy. This growth orientation can put unusual strains on management and can even force bad judgments if growth is advocated during periods when retrenchment is far more practical. In any event, unless management is committed to the attempt to make the company significantly larger in size and profitability and can do so in a planned and orderly way, a public offering is not likely to be a constructive move.

The headaches of a public company are many and annoying but not insurmountable. Remember that there are thousands of companies, listed and unlisted, that handle these problems in a routine fashion, and the rewards can be great. The Philip A. Hunt Chemical Company went public in February 1964 when the family sold 20% of the company for $1,200,000 (or a total value of $6 million). Subsequent public offerings and "144" sales permitted the family and its charities to realize several more millions of dollars. New capital raised through public sale of additional shares provided funds for expansion of sales from $10 million to over $60 million over a 10-year period. As of a recent date, the family sold the balance of its holdings to a British group for about $40 million.

Public ownership presents problems but offers perhaps the most effective way of continuing the growth pattern of an expanding company.

PERSPECTIVES

The relationship between the entrepreneur and the venture capitalist is often a critical factor in the success or failure of a new business development. To develop a productive, honest working relationship, it is helpful to recognize the biases, prejudices and pressure points that have emerged from the experiences of both venture capitalists and entrepreneurs. Understanding different viewpoints opens the communications channels needed to establish strong relationships.

Before investing in any management team, venture capitalists look for the right skills and disciplines, but they also look for a chemistry or "gut feeling" that gives them the personal go-ahead signal regarding management. This section examines the techniques employed by several professional venture capitalists in evaluating management teams and offers some valuable advice for the entrepreneur on early relationships with the venture capitalist.

Also presented is the view of an entrepreneur who has worked with, and established the respect of, a number of venture capitalists. His insights are valuable as a guide, and they place the entrepreneur/venture capitalist relationship in a unique perspective.

The Art of Venturing

FREDERICK R. ADLER

One of the secrets of successful venturing is to help managers to manage themselves. This is part of what the venture capitalist is paid to do, particularly if he is heavily engaged in startups, which is our primary activity. Picking a successful management team lies at the very heart of a successful venture capital investment. The problem is that identifying such talent is a very esoteric exercise to which there is no scientific approach.

One technique is to "psych out" the prospective management team. Try to get to know them in the best possible manner—not in a conference room, but on the floor of the plant. How do they function in periods of extreme pressure, the condition under which most small companies grow? How well are they going to survive under the pressure of meeting next week's payroll? Small comments often can provide a clue to management's thinking and capability, not as they relate merely to running a small company, but also to the creation and management of a large, rich company.

One aspect of this technique is to constantly monitor the quality of management's judgment. Make probes that are designed partly to aggravate or irritate a manager to see how he will react. Investigate potential flaws and weaknesses in the management structure. Often acquisition-hungry managers will try to cover up flaws in their own operation rather than develop a balanced business plan. If there are too many weaknesses, or if the weaknesses are too great, management stability is not going to be equal to management ambition, and the whole project will not make sense.

WARNING SIGNALS

There are some things said or positions taken by entrepreneurs in meetings that serve as major warning signals or at least indicate weakness in judgment.

"*There is nothing like this product on the market today.*" Generally this statement indicates that a man has not done his homework or that he may have designed a perfect product for a market that does not exist.

One of the major dangers with startups is that they often involve products for which the market is exceedingly difficult to assess. Venture capitalists rarely back totally new products. They usually back improvements on existing products, such as cases where a new manufacturing technique will reduce manufacturing costs. The Data General financing was only a startup from a technical viewpoint. The management team had designed computers and built software for Digital Equipment Corporation. They had designed and developed 12-bit, general-purpose small computers. Obviously there was no question that they could design and build a general-purpose computer for the new company. The question was, how good are these men going to be at managing their own business? Thus, the key risks were not product risks, although some new design techniques were employed; instead, they primarily related to marketing and management. The central question almost always comes down to whether the product can be sold, not whether it is the only such product on the market.

"*There isn't really a great widget available on the market today that will interchange with an existing piece of equipment.*" Often the product and development costs for a special piece of equipment that is fully interchangeable with other manufacturers' units are so excessive that the business will never be able to recoup the costs. Striving for perfection in a new product so that it is fully interchangeable with everything usually poses major problems, and it is far better to develop a good product, for which a real demand exists, that can be put into production at a reasonable cost.

Another major warning signal is an inordinate concern with salary, company cars, and other fringe benefits at the time of the original negotiation for financing. Venture capitalists hate to see money wasted, and particularly in a new enterprise, every dollar must be marshaled very carefully if the business is to be assured of survival. An entrepreneur's focus on such things as a car, the size of his office, travel expenses, and so forth, usually indicates a mental approach and lack of dedication that would divert his attention away from developing a major business success.

The man who is concerned about whether he will have full use of a secretary, a large car, and a 15' × 16' office, tends to be thinking more like an employee than a partner. He is not likely to be as concerned about how much money he spends to develop a product or to be concerned that his share of the equity is being dissipated by such high capital expenditures. The results can be very negative from the investor's point of view.

The Tortoise or Hare Approach

There are two ways of viewing a new project or startup venture. One is that it is of utmost importance to get into the market quickly with a new product to beat competitors. To accomplish this target, substantial additional monies often must be invested. The other alternative is to bring the product to market slowly and at the lowest possible price. Although the danger of competition due to lost time is increased, I lean toward the cheap side and tend to avoid early investment projects that are trying to beat the clock.

Management as a Popularity Contest

Another negative feature is exhibited by the manager who feels he is running a contest for the affection of his coworkers. The successful entrepreneur must step up and bite the bullet when critical decisions are required. When demand slacks, production must be cut and this means layoffs. Middle management must be used to the fullest possible extent to avoid overhead expenses under these conditions. Trying to keep all employees while hoping for the business to pick up can often be a disastrous strategy. The company may not be around by the time demand increases.

The Market Plunger

One petty irritation is the stock market approach—that is, the approach of a manager who spends much of his time being concerned with the price of relative equities of similar kinds of businesses. Moreover, managers who make presentations based on this type of analysis overprice their projects. One of the obvious tenets of profitable venturing is to attempt to gain entry into a new project at relatively low valuations, subject to the caveat that it pays to pay more for the really big play.

Shotgun Product Development

Another major problem is the failure of management to focus on the major objectives of the business. All venture capitalists have been exposed to managers who keep starting new product development programs and are unable to focus on the specific product that will make the company highly successful. The manager who proposes to work on ten products, even though they may be good ones, seldom develops the one excellent product from which the company can make a major success.

The Genius

Maybe someday I will meet "The Genius," but I doubt it. No man has the experience or time to be first-rate in everything. The smartest people are those who make use of the smartest people they know in order to get the job done. They use management personnel, bankers, venture capitalists, and anyone who can give them information or an advantage.

THE IDEAL ENTREPRENEUR

In a sense, every venture capitalist is looking for the man with management experience and profit and loss responsibility who is greedy, hungry, and yet honest and sincere. He must have the intellectual integrity to admit his mistakes and to recognize and reward other people's talents. This man must be technically qualified to do the job, but must not be so immersed in the technology that he loses sight of the need to build a profitable business rather than a bunch of fancy products. He must be a man of ego. If he does not have a very large ego, he is not going to view the obstacles with sufficient confidence. Yet if he is too egocentric and onesider, he will make some serious, dumb decisions because he refuses to take input from others.

The man must be tough enough to make very hard decisions if the venture is to survive, and that means firing his best friend if necessary. Yet he must be smart and mature enough so that this toughness is tempered and so that the people he needs around him will not leave because his attitudes irritate them.

The venture capital business is one of persistence. Every venture capital deal has experienced unexpected problems. They happen daily, weekly, or monthly, and there are enough big ones to scare every manager and venture capitalist. Good managements overcome these problems. The weaker ones fall by the wayside.

To be successful in developing a new project, management must be aggressive, but at the same time it cannot let ambition outstrip its pocketbook. A major problem in the venture business is that almost every early-stage project has a limited source of funds, unless it achieves instant success (a great rarity). Ambitions must be measured and desires reined in to the very tight limits of the pocketbook.

CHARACTERISTICS OF SUCCESSFUL PROJECTS

In our most successful investments, management has had a very close-working relationship, both financially and operationally, with our venture capital group. Senior management has tended to operate in a very open-minded, flexible, questioning way in order to obtain everyone's views. Exploring alternatives and brainstorming important decisions with all of the high-caliber people involved has been a key aspect in making sound management decisions.

Perhaps this is a contradiction of the theory of the great leader, but it may be that there is no such person. Generally speaking, it is interaction that produces good management decisions.

At Data General, the top management personnel are extremely capable and mature, and they run the company in every sense. Yet, in spite of my "non-involvement" with actual operations, we still find time to get together every few weeks. We talk at least three or four times a week. When there is nothing specific to discuss, we try to keep each other informed of everything that is or eventually could be a major problem. Again, I emphasize that our discussions do not cover day-to-day operations, which must be in the hands of competent management. But they do cover the broader policy and planning aspects of managing the business, particularly in finance, acquisitions, and senior personnel.

My observation is that people who are good managers take advantage of each other by interacting as much as possible. Building a company from a small base entails a world of mistakes, and the trick is to avoid those that are fatal. By talking to enough bright people, particularly those with direct experience in building a business, management should be able to avoid such mistakes. However, there are no supermen, and it is only by great effort and conscientious attention that businesses can be effectively managed during their earlier growth periods.

Pitfalls in Venturing

ALAN PATRICOF

MANAGEMENT ATTITUDES

Management evaluation is most often the critical component of the venture investment decision process and our experience has brought about strong prejudices regarding management attitudes. We are biased against management teams on which nobody serves as president; that is, three men working together, equally sharing one-third of the equity of the business, and making committee decisions. Situations like this often create problems, and we prefer to finance projects in which a balanced management team will be presented but where one man is clearly the president. We don't like general managers who assume only limited responsibilities.

The Patricof organization is also prejudiced against managements that are unwilling to put what we feel is a significant amount of their own money into an existing project. Generally, anyone who has the capability to be president of the type of business that interests us would have accumulated enough capital to make a significant investment. It is not the amount of money that is critical, however, but rather that it demonstrates total commitment for the entrepreneur. It is too easy for management personnel to walk away from a project that is turning sour if a significant amount of their own capital is not being risked.

At the inception of a business, the entrepreneur should rely most heavily on capital from personal and related sources such as friends, relatives, suppliers, and customers to start the business and develop the product and management team. Then six months or a year later, a business should be in a more favorable position to attract professional venture capital funding. It might be appropriate for the entrepreneur to sound our venture capitalists before going through the first stage to see if the project will be sufficiently interesting once it has come to life.

One of the great problems of financing startups arises when one considers that some of the principal members of the starting management group may turn out to be ineffective. With a significant percentage of the equity allocated to those individuals there is normally no way of buying back these positions during the early stages, and future financing of the company can become very difficult. For example, take the case of a vice-president of marketing who is not effective in spearheading the company's sales effort and must be removed from office. With perhaps 20% of the company granted to this individual at its inception, only 80% of the equity would be available to split among ongoing contributors to the business. The net result is that investors and both the new and old active and effective management find their equity positions diluted by someone who is unproductive. This problem is serious, but it can be resolved through buyback agreements, performance standards, and other remedies developed at the inception of the company.

Aside from these organizational and financial considerations, we are also interested in some personal facets of the entrepreneur's endeavor. Have the members of the management team known each other for some time? Have they worked together before? Is management truly dedicated to the business?

In one of the companies we were backing, management personnel often slept in the plant when major problems were developing. This is the kind of dedication that can mean the difference between the success and failure of a small business. Of course, this effort takes a tremendous toll on the entrepreneur's personal relationships. This is one of the major risks involved in starting a new business which entrepreneurs must recognize in advance.

WHY IT TAKES TIME TO MAKE AN INVESTMENT

We have found that it is extremely important to intimately know the people being financed, and to establish communication and understanding as early in the relationship as possible. The more time the venture capitalist spends with the entrepreneur, the better he can assess capabilities, vision, ambition, and the other key qualities required to be successful. The longer we have to work with potential portfolio companies and their managements, the more comfortable we are when the time for investment arises.

Businesses that must raise money yesterday to keep the business alive often start from below ground zero. They simply put too much pressure on the venture capitalist and do not give sufficient time to know and understand either management or the company. Furthermore, this indication of a lack of planning certainly reflects badly on management skills.

In terms of the positive aspect of management, the first characteristic to look for might be a lack of undue concern over salary. The president who is reasonable about salary income commands attention, but some demands indicate a life style and shortsightedness that may be counterproductive to small business development. It is far more important for the entrepreneur to worry about making $5 million from equity appreciation and hold salary levels to a reasonable minimum. In other words, do not start a company to get a raise.

Capital is one of the most precious commodities for a small company and cannot be wasted by high salaries, either in actual or philosophical terms. To generate major capital gains, management must make a number of major sacrifices, and salary is clearly one of them.

SOME DO'S AND DON'TS FOR THE ENTREPRENEUR

In presenting the company to the venture capitalist, do not let a third person do the selling. Company support personnel must not be allowed to crowd the meetings. Avoid bringing lawyers and accountants to the early meetings. At the initial stage, bring only the number two person. Better yet, initial contacts should be between only the venture capitalist and the president.

Be sure that the project lends itself to outside investors. Many excellent businesses have fairly limited growth potential even though they often can generate large earnings. They may not, however, be suited to public ownership or ownership by a large corporation, and generally these kinds of businesses will not be attractive to professional venture capitalists.

Another major problem for venture investors is the entrepreneur who tries to hold out for the largest amount of equity at the lowest terms. Don't create this sort of obstacle. Any number of valid projects have never gotten off the ground because the entrepreneur simply did not understand the wages of capital—the percentage of equity that venture capitalists themselves view as a fair compensation for their risk. A few equity percentage points here and there in early-stage developments are relatively insignificant, but unreasonable negotiations can effect future relationships. Once the company begins to show progress, it is always possible to get options, to borrow money and buy stock at low prices, buy a percentage of the venture capitalist's position, or take a number of steps that would create major capital gains potential. This is a critical decision that must be made and the good entrepreneur must know when he is fairly close to the best deal he can get and settle for that.

WHAT KIND OF PERSON SHOULD ATTEMPT TO BUILD A COMPANY?

Most people do not have the confidence to run their own companies. One of the greatest traps that the unwary can fall into is to try to be a company president without having the capability. It is an exceedingly difficult task to start a new company. The responsibilities are awesome. The time commitments are immense. The personal price that must be paid in terms of family relationships is extreme. Tensions are enormous because problems can be endless.

Many times these problems have not been experienced in any other business relationship. There will be any number of crises when the business will appear to fail or seriously falter. It will often be necessary to raise additional capital during these periods and management must have great amounts of fortitude, exceptional optimism tempered with realism, an overwhelming desire to succeed, great strength of character and leadership, and qualities such as specific technical skills in marketing, product development, and other specific areas.

Another characteristic that is important even though it tends to contradict those just mentioned is flexibility. The successful entrepreneur must know if a product or approach to a market is not working and will not work, and must have the flexibility to go back to the drawing board, redesign the product, develop a new marketing strategy, and so forth. In other words, there is a critical difference between having the fortitude to push through a valid plan and being sufficiently aware to know when a plan is not valid and must be redirected and redeveloped. This is an area that often traps a management since it is one of the most intangible aspects of the business arena.

Anyone thinking of reaching out for the American dream to start a major enterprise should do a thorough self-evaluation to be confident of the qualities necessary to insure the project through to its ultimate success.

The Entrepreneur's Perspective

DONALD J. KRAMER

After a technical-type high school education, I started college in engineering, which I soon found I hated and consequently only lasted six months. Joining the Navy for four years gave me a different type of education, learning about people, and I came out with an incredible passion to succeed. Back in college, I graduated number one in my class majoring in accounting at Northeastern University, and was accepted at graduate school. With family responsibilities, however, eating became the most important habit to satisfy, so I went to work, although I did ultimately get my MBA from a combination of study at Syracuse University and Boston University.

My career path has been a progression from big companies to small, and I soon became a small business addict. Smaller business management is my narcotic. I am hooked and would find it difficult to go back to larger companies' bureaucratic structures. My first exposure to the world of venture capital came when I helped form a new facsimile company in the late 1960s with a corporate sponsor for funding and technology. This was a noteworthy failure for me and for my meager savings which I had invested, although I learned more from that failure than from a lot of subsequent successes. After a typically euphoric two years, we were asked to sell the business when the parent had some problems. We successfully sold it five times and every time the parent's assessment of the value went up until the parent decided it was so good they would keep it. I decided to move on, but I learned that one of the most important keys to business success is to understand the objectives and motivations of the business' investors.

ABOUT VENTURE CAPITALISTS

The primary importance of venture capitalists to an entrepreneur is MONEY, and they all have money, but investors do differ in objectives, motivations, and capabilities. The relationship between operating management and the business' outside investors can help or harm a business' development. Understanding objectives is the first way to help that relationship. During the negotiation process the objectives should be uncovered.

Corporate venture capitalists may have entirely different objectives from the financial orientation of most venture investors. Corporations may only be interested in research and development off the balance sheet or off the P & L statements. I am generally uncomfortable with corporate investors because their objectives and mine are likely to be quite different.

The majority of individual venture capitalists are personally compensated on the basis of the success of their portfolios and most pools, if not all, have a finite life. As venture partnerships end, they are primarily seeking return as opposed to new investments. It is important to understand where the potential investor is in that life cycle, and whether they intend to put together another fund with similar objectives. One has to recognize that these objectives can change due to money market changes, liquidity needs, or what have you. Perhaps the initial objective can be laid out, but the ultimate comfort that they are never going to change cannot be made.

In initial dealings with venture capitalists, they will check on your background and references and it is just as important for you to do the same to them. It is perfectly reasonable to ask for references from those who may invest in you. Next, there is the personal chemistry—a very important factor. This must be seen and felt early since future events and problems will strain most relationships. Find out whether or not they have the necessary skills to assist you in *your* particular venture. Lastly, remind yourself that they are the stockholders, they do, in fact, own the company.

Venture capitalists are all different and each fund is different. Some are very good at startups, but there are probably fewer of those than any other kind. In my opinion, this requires operating skills in order to help a new management over some rough spots. Usually a company cannot afford to hire all the talent it needs, it has to get advice and there are times when a venture capitalist can provide this. Many differences depend on where they get their money and whether they are looking for an incremental percentage return, whether they hope to shoot the moon, whether they are in for five years or forever.

People have different skills and venture capitalists are no different. Some are good technically, although they are rare. There are not too many good marketers—even though most all venture capitalists think they are because marketing is relatively easy to understand. I find whenever I get into a box with a venture capitalist, I start talking "bits and bytes," even though I do not know them, because it usually backs them off. They do not understand it either. A few venture capitalists are aware of technical aspects, most feel they understand the marketing but the only thing they really understand is venture capital. They know what kind of a deal will sell and to whom it will sell.

Venture firms tend to hire very bright guys out of graduate schools in their late twenties, smart as hell, and hard working, but at least half of them do not know a thing initially. They get on a board of directors and end up getting on-the-job training. Sometimes, they can be very counterproductive. The problem is that they are so bright. If they were stupid, they would be easy to deal with—you'd just blow them away. But you can't. They've got a gem of an idea or they have unshakable curiosity and you'll end up conducting a lecture and a training session.

Every venture guy thinks he is a strategist. I disagree with a number of venture philosophies and one of them is "strategic thinking." So many of them have been educated in the two or three top business schools that they all think alike—not necessarily correctly, but alike. I don't believe that a small business should search for the perfect strategy. By sorting out the unattractive alternatives, you will be left with six or seven viable strategies—pick one and execute the hell out of it. Success in small business is not in having the perfect strategy; it is in the execution of a fundamentally sound strategy.

The venture people who are particularly good in the strategic sense have a very deep knowledge of a particular market. You cannot come up with a workable strategy without such understanding. If you are dealing with a lot of companies and industries, I don't care how bright you think you are, you cannot have an in-depth knowledge of all of them. Some venture capitalists can be very helpful in particular companies, but they cannot be all things to all people. The match between the knowledge and skill of the venture investors and the operating management is very important.

THE KISS PRINCIPLE
("KEEP IT SIMPLE, STUPID!")

Managing a small business has enough problems and we do not need the complexities that often are introduced by venture investors. I have frequently wondered why venture capitalists put a whole bunch of terms and conditions in a deal. Some things are logical, such as preemptive rights, registration rights, board seats, or observer positions. There is a tendency, however, on the part of lawyers of venture capitalists, to put in many other things which complicate a deal.

I think control is overplayed by entrepreneurs. No matter who has control—whatever that means—if there isn't an accommodation so that the "control" and the "non-control" can get together at some point, the business is in trouble and you have a more fundamental problem than control. The guy that runs the business has control, even if he doesn't own any stock. The entrepreneur that always searches and reaches for control either doesn't understand reality or has an immense ego, or both. From my point of view, I don't really worry too much about control, because if I don't like what they want me to do, I will leave and go do something else.

I run companies for people, if they don't like the way I run it they ought to get somebody else. I have no problem with that at all. I always tell some of the key investors, the day you don't like the way I am doing things, tell me. I am not going to be upset and will help you find my replacement and I can get another job. I get aggravated at managements that are only concerned about preserving their own position. What else is the issue of control except for that concern?

I think the relevance of control is not control but rather that it implies you have a bigger percentage. But what does this have to do with your ability to run a company's day-to-day operations? I would rather own 1% of something than 10% of nothing.

Structuring and pricing a deal should be kept as simple as possible. Pricing in an early-stage deal is not particularly important, except as it affects future relationships. When potential buyers in a second-round financing say, "I wish I had been around three years ago when the price was $1 rather than now at $6," I say, "Hey, you are not going to make the big bread on the spread between $1 and $6. If that is what you are satisfied with, I better not do the deal. You should be looking for the spread between $6 and $100." Pricing in second- and later-round financings is more important and it is clearer because you have something to measure it against. You can compare it to other companies in similar businesses or similar size companies in different businesses or both of these. What can you really evaluate a startup against?

My experience with Modicon was nice and simple, just common stock and we managed to stay that way. Hendrix, when I arrived, was complicated with all sorts of structures. There were too many venture capitalists in the company with diverse objectives. You had to deal with each separately. Each would sit around the table and negotiate the deal. First, venture capital Firm A needed a high interest rate and you would give it to them. Then venture capital Firm B needed a lower conversion, so you would give it to them. Someone else needed registration rights or other provisions and on and on and on. By the time it finally worked out you had a very complex deal with crazy anti-dilution provisions. We had common stock, three types of preferred stock, and convertible debentures. Everybody had different agreements, and I couldn't go to the bathroom without checking with somebody.

Finally, I tossed in the towel and wrote my investors a letter which said, "Dear People: I am not paying interest; we don't have the money. We are loaned up at the bank and drastically need a recapitalization." While my first suggestion was turned down, we finally arrived at another alternative which was accepted by the stockholders in the longest running stockholder meeting in the world—about four months. When the smoke blew away I had two fresh venture investors, the more disenchanted of the old investors were out, and I had gained a simplified capital structure. From that point on we were able to work our way through business problems without creating investor dissatisfaction.

I would much rather operate through a lead investor then with a big group of investors. A lead investor, however, must truly be a lead and have the confidence of other investors. In one of my situations there was a lead investor but the followers came to the meetings with their assistants. The board meetings were incredible —15 to 18 people there. Even this would have been OK if they would have just observed. The unfortunate thing is that most venture capitalists are smart, they have good ideas and have large egos, so the meeting ends up being a graduate seminar. The company may be dying but they will argue about some theoretical idea. Having venture capitalists on the board is fine and often constructive, but too many of them can be counterproductive.

Many venture capitalists do not take board seats but instead come as observers. The trouble with an observer role is that they have to realize they are there to observe. At one of my first Hendrix board meetings I had to rent a hall to fit everybody in and that became a little bit awkward. We had everyone and their brothers with a right to come and bring a friend, so it wasn't one on one; it was two or three or four on one. When we would have a vote I would occasionally see a hand up there that didn't belong and say, "Hey, wait a minute, you don't get a vote," and the hand would disappear. Actually, the observer role can work and be very effective if people contribute at the right time and in the right place. Under any business structures and with any relationship it is the effort put out to make things work that will build lasting relationships.

THE VENTURE CAPITALISTS/ ENTREPRENEUR RELATIONSHIP

Getting venture capital is like getting married—you wake up the next morning and the honeymoon is over. In a venture-backed situation the honeymoon is generally a very short period—it usually ends at the closing.

Too many entrepreneurs forget who owns the company. The stockholders own the company. The chief executive is an owner only in the sense of his stock ownership and he must subjugate himself as an employee to himself as a stockholder and to the other stockholders. While he may be president, perhaps chief executive officer, he is still an employee. Those other people, some of whom are venture capitalists, own the company and they can tell him whatever they want him to do.

The venture capitalists, by and large, have a very important fiduciary responsibility. They are responsible for investing their client's money for financial gain and they have a right to expect a certain level of performance. I don't find that offensive at all, but I think some entrepreneurs do. If your stockholder venture capitalists want to sell the company and you don't, then it is reasonable to argue. If your argument is based on future growth, maybe you have a valid point. But, if it is because you don't want to work for a big company, I think you are way off base.

I did not want to sell Modicon to anyone at that particular time. The company was moving nicely and I felt we had far more to gain by remaining independent. Some owners, however, had other considerations and this was their prerogative. This was an opportunity for them to realize substantial financial gains and why should management stand in their way? Gould was an excellent choice overall, as long as the desire was to sell. As a matter of fact, I enjoyed working for Gould and was given additional responsibilities that would not have been available to me with Modicon as an independent company. The small business narcotic, however, brought me back to Hendrix.

If a venture investor had a strong conviction differing from my own, I would argue with them as I would argue with any boss— if I felt it important. If my boss finally said, "I want it done such and so," I would then decide whether I could do it or not. If no was the answer, I would say you ought to get someone else who can do it, because I can't support your position. I don't present that as a threat to the venture capitalists, just a statement of fact. If a venture capitalist feels so strongly about a particular strategy and cannot sell the idea to management, then he ought to change the management and get someone else to do it his way. But it is a mistake for the venture capitalist to get into that mode, especially since egos must be bruised in admitting a mistake in selecting the original management.

A venture capitalist must sell his ideas and not all of them are willing to do that. They are in a poor position to produce edicts since they are not going to be the ones to execute the strategy or the ideas—this is management's responsibility. They ought to play more of a board member role, dealing with general strategies not details.

I get exceptionally annoyed at directors' meetings where a venture capitalist confuses director and stockholder roles. As a director he has an individual responsibility to the company and all stockholders, not to the venture fund. If he wants to be a stockholder and argue from a stockholder's point of view he ought to call a stockholder meeting. You cannot mix these two roles. Good people, to a large degree, can divorce or separate those two functions, but many venture guys sitting on boards are unable to separate their venture investment objectives from the company's objectives. My response to this problem is to point out that at a board meeting, you only get one vote whether you own 10% or 99% or nothing. If you want a stockholders meeting go call one. If you want to run the whole company then buy the company and do whatever the hell you want.

The magic of successfully dealing with venture capitalists is mutual confidence. They have to have confidence in you and, if so, 95% of the problems never occur. How do you develop this confidence? It is doing what you say you are going to do. A cynic might say that venture capitalists are only concerned with numbers and, perhaps, this may be true in a minor way because how else can the score be kept. It is more important, however, that you can accurately predict the course of the business than it is to make an immediate profit. Reliable forecasting gives the venture capitalist confidence in your ability to understand your markets, your technology, and your business.

An entrepreneur or a chief executive has to understand his employees, his markets, his technology, and his responsibilities. But he also has to understand his stockholders and venture capitalists have objectives which must be considered. If you want venture capital then you have to accept the fact that venture capitalists have objectives which are independent of your individual empire. If one doesn't want to be subjected to those factors, don't get the venture money. If you are smart, go get the money somewhere else.

Entrepreneurs make a mistake when they say "give me his money and I can get along with him." A state of siege between management and owners will hurt a company's development. But, in the final analysis, if the company is dying and needs the money, take the money, because living badly is better than dying. If you can't live with the owners, then it may be best to find new management that can work with them so your ownership position may be built into greater value while you do something else. It is easier to change management than to change stockholders. A company is in business to be successful, and it is the relationships between people that make this happen.

The Relationship Between Venture Capitalist and Entrepreneur

BROOK H. BYERS

Venture capital portfolio monitoring might be compared to farming; that is, there are many different techniques employed between seed planting and the harvest. No single method is perfect, because characteristics, such as the strength of the plant, the abilities of the farmer, and the weather in current season, must be considered in each case. The venture capital investor must decide for each investment what to do in the years between the intensive period of analysis and negotiation leading to an investment and the future period when capital may be withdrawn and a return on investment realized. This decision depends on the type of involvement an investor seeks; some prefer to rely on management reports and periodic company visits, while others prefer to become "working partners" with management.

Our preference at KPC&B is for significant involvement—giving business counsel and emotional support to the company and receiving enhancement of our investment and personal satisfaction in return.

FACTORS AFFECTING MONITORING

Each investment deserves a unique monitoring approach, which depends on several key factors affecting our relationship with the company, including:

- the length of time we plan to be invested,
- the company's need for assistance,
- management's willingness to accept advice,
- the portion of our total portfolio invested in the company,
- our expertise relative to company needs,
- our time commitments and the company's location,
- the characteristics of co-investors, and
- the degree of potential influence on the company because of both percentage of ownership and, very importantly, personal relationships with management.

Based on such factors, we tailor a monitoring method for each investment by using a combination of the following roles: director, interim officer, ad hoc volunteer, active manager, fire extinguisher, project consultant, retained consultant, and lecturer. The tailored combination changes significantly over the life of the investment.

A CASE EXAMPLE OF THIS APPROACH

In 1967, AMC led a group of venture capital investors, who had participated in several previous deals together, into a $150,000 equity financing of an electronics manufacturer (called Spectrum Corporation in this article). In that year, Spectrum's annual sales were under $400,000 with substantial losses. Spectrum planned to market a new device, which was to serve the expected boom in new applications. The investor group finalized the deal in late 1967 and put two members on a five-man board, which chose an AMC staff member as chairman.

In early 1968, Spectrum began experiencing difficulties in engineering and in product returns from customers. Near the middle of 1968, the board of directors determined that the president was unable to manage the technical and marketing problems of Spectrum. He was let go, and the AMC board member became president and chief executive officer. For the next few months, our man commuted the hour's drive to and from Spectrum almost daily, working on production problems, soothing angry customers, and searching for a permanent president.

In the fall of 1968, we heard of an outstanding entrepreneur who wanted financing for his company, which marketed related products with an excellent brand name. By early 1969, our man had negotiated a merger of the two companies, with the entrepreneur as the new president and the original Spectrum investor group refinancing the deal with an additional $200,000.

Throughout 1969, the AMC staff member continued to visit Spectrum two to four times a month to assist with management decisions and financial planning. By 1970, Spectrum required another round of financing, so our man initiated and negotiated a $350,000 investment by a large New York venture capital fund.

Throughout 1971, 1972, and 1973, he visited Spectrum about twice each month to assist the management in pricing discussions, planning for profitability, employee relations, and liaison with investors. He also occasionally traveled for the company to visit trade shows and to negotiate with potential marketing representatives and suppliers, both foreign and domestic. Crises sometimes occurred, such as when Spectrum's bank canceled its line of credit. Our man initiated discussions and helped negotiate a favorable deal with a major California bank, which is still the company's lender.

As Spectrum became profitable and began to grow rapidly, its ongoing problems evolved from operations and risk finance to marketing and development of management depth. Our man provided assistance to the management in policy decisions and in financial planning. AMC helped negotiate an additional $500,000 for working capital in 1974 from a major southwestern venture capital group and provided counseling when Spectrum contemplated an acquision of another company.

Throughout this eight-year involvement, AMC contributed a significant amount of time, received minor compensation, but was reimbursed for expenses. However, it is our belief that Spectrum would not be worth its value today, or maybe not even have survived, if this portfolio monitoring approach had not been implemented. Furthermore, we know that these experiences contribute significantly to our own professional and personal development.

In its fiscal 1975 year, Spectrum exceeded $14 million in revenues and $1.2 million in profits after full taxes with continuing rapid growth expected. The company "went public" in 1976 at a price over 10 times the average cost to the venture capital investors and management.

BENEFITS OF THIS APPROACH

We use the "significant involvement" approach to monitoring primarily because we believe it gives us *greater investment success*. However, many other benefits accrue to us, including:

1. Greater personal satisfaction in haivng taken an active role in the growth of a new business,
2. Professional training in business and technology from the "scar tissue" of being involved,
3. Being "in pace" with the company if top management changes are needed,
4. Intimate familiarity with the investment when later financings or sellouts are proposed, and
5. The ability to attract venture capital investors (and their capital) from other geographical regions, who may also desire a local, "watchdog" investor.

Benefits accrue to our companies and aid in our investment success because we provide:

1. A sounding board for top management on a personal level with non-employees,
2. Broad contacts for diversification, joint ventures, foreign marketing, banking, and consultants with special skills,
3. Independence for specific projects, such as strategic plans, acquisitions, compensation plans, and top management screening,

4. Arrangements for orderly private equity financings, and
5. Communications with the investment community before and after a public offering.

PROBLEMS OF THIS APPROACH

We sometimes experience problems because of our "significant involvement" monitoring method. Among these problems are the following:

1. Involvement requires time, which can mean harder work by investors or an increase in staff—usually the former, however, because of the low overhead nature of the venture capital business.
2. Direct expenses are sometimes not reimbursed, especially by newer companies.
3. Some managers are slow to accept significant investor involvement, viewing it as an intrusion upon their authority.
4. Once trust is established with management and the involvement is mutually satisfying, some entrepreneurs expect unlimited sponsorship by the investor.
5. It is sometimes difficult to distinguish non-recurring problems (appropriate for our approach) from recurring problems (the operating responsibilities of management).
6. "Quiet" investment partners sometimes place a *de facto* responsibility for the investment on active investors.
7. An investor, because of significant involvement, is often obligated to participate in later equity financings, because such participation will determine the success of the offering, even though one might personally prefer not to participate further than a present investment level.
8. An involved investor can lose objectivity about an investment and make mistakes in the timing of selling as to when the venture capital investment has achieved relative maturity and one's ownership should be transferred to another level of sponsorship.

SUMMARY

We believe that investing capital in venture situations, combined with involved assistance as described in this article, offers both above average investment returns and better chances for survival of new companies in their difficult early years.

Index

acquisition financing, 5
addresses to obtain information on: CDCs, 65; EDCs, 70; MESBICs, 76; SBICs, 55
advertising, 105, 206–17
Appalachian Regional Commission (ARC), 69
Appropriate Technology Grants Program (Department of Energy), 38

background on raising venture capital, 7–26
balance sheet forecasts, 118–19
Baltimore, venture capital firms in, 34
banker, investment, selection of, 201–3
bank-related SBICs, 59
Boston, venture capital firms in, 34, 35

business expansion. *See* expansion financing
business plan, 20–22, 89–91, 97–98, 179; preparing, 95–120
business startups. *See* startup financing
buyout, leveraged. *See* leveraged buyout financing

California, venture capital firms in, 34–35, 49–50; for high-technology ventures, 34–35, 49–50; for startup financing, 35
cash flow forecast, 116–18, 119
CDCs. *See* Community Development Corporations
Chicago, venture capital firms in, 34
Commerce Technical Advisory Board, 43
common stock. *See* stock

249

Community Development Corporations (CDCs): description, 63–69; flexibility of, 63, 67; geographic restrictions, 63, 65; locations, obtaining list of, 65
Community Services Administration, 64, 65
competition, assessing, 102–3
computer companies, investments in, 31, 79
Connecticut (southern), venture capital firms in, 34
Connecticut Product Development Corporation, 38
control, 131, 135–36, 237–38; ownership, relation to, 92, 127
convertible debentures. *See* debentures
convertible preferred stock. *See* stock
corporations as venture capital sources: capital commitments, 30, 33, 79; corporate motives, 77, 235; description, 33–34, 77–83; history, 78–79; number of, 33, 79; selecting, 81–82
critical risks assessment, 113

Dallas, venture capital firms in, 34, 35
debentures: documents and terms, 127–28, 172–74; MESBIC, 74; SBIC, 56, 58
Department of Commerce, 38, 70, 73
design and development plans, 106–7, 180

early stage financing, 9, 31, 47; definition, 3–4; first-stage, 4, 47, 56; seed, *see* seed financing; startup, *see* startup financing

East Coast venture capital firms, 34–35
Economic Development Commissions (EDCs): description, 69–70; flexibility of, 63; geographic restrictions, 63, 65; information on, obtaining, 70
EDCs. *See* Economic Development Commissions
employment agreements, 175
Energy Related Inventions Program, 38
energy ventures, EDC funding for, 70
engineering management ability, evaluation of, 23–24
entrepreneurs: single, disadvantages of, 15; successful, characteristics of, 15–26, 226–27, 232–33; vs. venture capitalist, 136–37, 223–28, 234–48
expansion financing, 4, 9, 12, 31; obtaining, 41–43; stock, offering, *see* going public
Experimental Technology Incentives Program, 38

financial instruments, 128–30
financial management ability, evaluation of, 24
financial plan, 114–19
financial public relations, 206–17
financing: instruments, 128–30; legal documents, 157–77; obtaining, *see* raising venture capital; pricing, 144–56; structuring, 134–44
firms, venture capital: capital commitments, 13, 30; CDCs, *see* Community Development Corporations; choosing, 5–6, 88, 91–92; corporate subsid-

Index /251

iaries, *see* corporations as venture capital sources; dealing with, guidelines, 87–94, 136–37, 223–28, 234–48; EDCs, *see* Economic Development Commissions; financing, obtaining from, *see* raising venture capital; as a general resource, 75, 87, 93–94, 176, 243–48; government attitude toward, 14; history, 10–14; independent, 2, 10–14, 30–32; inventors, disinterest in, 37; MESBICs, *see* Minority Enterprise Small Business Investment Companies; number of, 6, 13, 31, 39; overview, 9–14, 29–35; private, 2, 10–14, 30–32; profit targets, 145–46; SBICs, *see* Small Business Investment Companies; seed financing, disinterest in, 47; startups, disinterest in, 39
first-stage financing, 4, 47, 57. *See also* early stage financing
fourth-stage financing, 4

geographic considerations, 34–35, 63, 65; in business plan, 107; diminishing importance of, 35
going public: example, 203–5; financial public relations, 206–17; guide to, 197–205; history, 196, 197; management needs, change in, 218–20
government funding sources: CDCs, *see* Community Development Corporations; EDCs, *see* Economic Development Commissions; grants, 38, 49; MESBICs, *see* Minority Enterprise Small Business Investment Companies; overview, 2, 38; SBICs, *see* Small Business Investment Companies; state programs, 38
grant programs, 38, 49
growth, financing. *See* expansion financing

high-technology investments: by corporations, 33–34, 77, 78; by independent firms, 31, 37–38, 49–50; from public sources, 32, 38, 49
Houston, venture capital firms in, 34, 35

ideas for ventures seeking financing, 37, 99–100, 227–28; acceptance, odds of, 20–22; design and development plans, 106–7, 180; early stage financing of, *see* early stage financing
independent venture capital firms, 2, 10–14, 30–32
informal investors, 36–46
instrument companies, investments in, 79
instruments, financial, 128–30
inventors, 37–38
investment banker, selection of, 201–3

labor force, 65–66, 109
legal documents, guide to, 157–77
legal skills, evaluation of, 26
leveraged buyout financing, 9, 31, 33; definition, 5; examples, 189–92; principles, 187–89; SBIC, 58
liquidity, 130–32, 135
loans. *See* debentures

Maine Capital Corporation, 38
management assistance to venture

capital clients, 75, 87, 93–94, 176, 243–48
management buyout financing. *See* leveraged buyout financing
management of businesses seeking venture capital: assessment of, 16–20, 22–26, 179–80, 187–93, 223–24, 229–30; describing in business plan, 109–11; describing in presentation, 123–24; functions, 22–26; publicly held companies, 218–20. *See also* entrepreneurs
market, identifying, 31, 101–5, 123, 181–83
market, new, corporate interest in, 77
marketing ability, evaluation of, 22–23
Massachusetts Technology Development Corporation, 38
medical electronics companies, investments in, 79
merger partners, 83
MESBICs. *See* Minority Enterprise Small Business Investment Companies
Minneapolis, venture capital firms in, 34, 35
Minority Business Enterprise, Department of, 73
Minority Enterprise Small Business Investment Companies (MESBICs): capital in, 33, 72, 73; description, 2, 72–76; information on, obtaining, 76; number of, 33, 73

National Association of Small Business Investment Companies (NASBIC), 35, 42
National Bureau of Standards Energy Related Inventions Program, 38
National Science Foundation grants, 38, 49
National Venture Capital Association (NVCA), 35, 39
natural resources development ventures, EDC funding for, 70
New England state investment sources, 38
New York City, venture capital firms in, 34

operations management ability, evaluation of, 23
operations plan, 107–9
ownership, 129–30; control, relation to, 92, 127

Pacific Northwest, venture capital firms in, 34, 49–50
partnerships, tax-shelter oriented, 49–50
pension funds, 29, 31
personnel management ability, evaluation of, 25–26
piggyback registrations, 169–70
preferred stock. *See* stock
presentation of proposal to venture capitalists, 121–26, 231
pre-startup financing. *See* seed financing
pricing the financing, 144–56
pricing the product, 104–5
private venture capital sources, 2, 10–14, 30–32
products: design and development plans, 106–7, 180; pricing, 104–5. *See also* ideas for ventures seeking financing
profit and loss forecast, 114–16

Index /253

profit targets of venture capitalists, 145–46
promotion, 105, 206–17
public relations, 105, 206–17
public venture capital sources, 2–3, 218–20. *See also* government funding sources
purchase agreement, 158–71

raising venture capital: background, 7–26; business development stages, *see* early stage financing, expansion financing, leveraged buyout financing; business plan, *see* business plan; case history, 178–86; CDCs, *see* Community Development Corporations; from corporations, *see* corporations as venture capital sources; from EDCs, *see* Economic Development Commissions; example of amounts required, 51, 178–86; from firms, *see* firms, venture capital; geographic considerations, 34–35, 63, 65, 107; from government, *see* government funding sources; how to, 85–193, 223–28; from individuals, *see* informal investors ; legal documents, guide to, 157–77; from MESBICs, *see* Minority Enterprise Small Business Investment Companies ; overview, 2–6, 9–14; presentation, 121–26, 231; pricing, 144–56; public sources, 2–3, 218 20, *see also* government funding sources; purchase agreement, 158–71; from SBICs, *see* Small Business Investment Companies; from Small Business

Administration, 54–62; sources, 27–83; steps to take, 85–193; structuring, 134–44; terms, familiarity with, 127–28, 172–74
recreation ventures, EDC funding for, 70
registration rights, 130
research and development: contract income, 83; management ability, evaluation of, 23–24; partnerships, 49–50
risks assessment, 113
Rule 144, 128–29, 170

sales ability, evaluation of, 22–23
sales methods, 105. *See also* market, identifying
San Francisco, venture capital firms in, 34–35, 49–50
SBA. *See* Small Business Administration
SBICs. *See* Small Business Investment Companies
schedule for venture, 111–12
second-stage financing, 4, 57, 75
securities. *See* stock
Securities and Exchange Commission (SEC), 130, 200, 201, 204, 205, 207, 212
seed financing, 9, 31; definition, 3–4; obtaining, 47–53; rarity of, 47; and startup financing, 48–49
self-evaluation of management skills, 16–20, 22–26
service business investments, 31
sinking funds, 132
Small Business Administration (SBA), 45, 54–62; guaranteed loans, 60–62; MESBICs, *see* Minority Enterprise Small Busi-

ness Investment Companies;
SBICs, *see* Small Business
Investment Companies
Small Business Innovation Research Program (SBIR), 38
Small Business Investment Act of
1958, 10
Small Business Investment Companies (SBICs): capital commitments, 30, 32; description,
2, 32–33, 54–60; financing,
types of, 32–33, 55–60; history,
10–11; list of, obtaining, 55;
number of, 32, 55
Small Business Participating
Debenture, 42–43
Southeast, venture capital firms
in, 34
southern California, venture
capital firms in, 34, 49–50
specialty SBICs, 60
startup financing, 9, 31, 47; capital
commitments, 39; definition, 4;
disinterest of firms in, 39; obtaining, 39–41, 57; pricing,
148–49; and seed financing,
48–49
state funding programs, 38
stock: common, description of,
128; MESBIC purchase, 74;
offering, *see* going public; preferred, description of, 128;
purchase warrant agreement,
172, 173–74, 176; SBIC purchase, 56, 58; terms used, 127–
28, 129; venture capital firm
purchase, 134–35, 137–44,
149–50
St. Paul, venture capital firms in,
34, 35
structuring financing, 134–44
subsidiaries, venture capital. *See*
corporations as venture capital
sources

tax skills, evaluation of, 26
technology-based investments. *See*
high-technology investments
telecommunications companies,
investments in, 79
terms, financing, familiarity with,
127–28, 172–74
third-stage financing, 4, 57, 75
tourism, EDC funding for, 70
transportation ventures, EDC
funding for, 70
turn-around financing, SBIC, 58

United States government departments and agencies. *See* specific
name (e.g., *Small Business
Administration*)

venture capital: definition, 9–10;
industry, *see* firms, venture
capital; informal, 36–46; private, 2, 10–14, 30–32; public,
2–3, 218–20, *see also* government funding sources; raising,
see raising venture capital;
subsidiaries, *see* corporations as
venture capital sources
venture capitalists. *See* firms,
venture capital; informal investors

warrant, stock purchase, 172,
173–74, 176
Washington, D.C., venture capital
firms in, 34
West Coast, venture capital firms
on, 34, 35, 49–50
"window on technology" concept,
34, 78